A Journey of Riches

The Benefit of Challenge

John Spender

First published by Motionmediainternational 2017

Copyright c 2017 John Spender

ISBN:978-0994498359

The publisher specifically disclaims responsibility for any adverse consequences, which may result from use of the information contained herein. Permission to use information has been sought by the author. Any breaches will be rectified in further editions of the book.

All rights reserved. No part of this publication may be reproduced, stored in or introduced into a retrieval system, or transmitted in any form, or by any means (electronic, mechanical, photocopying, recording or otherwise) without the prior written permission of the author. Any person who does any unauthorised act in relation to this publication may be liable to criminal prosecution and civil claims for damages. Enquiries should be made through the publisher.

Cover design: MotionMediaInternational

Layout and typesetting: MotionMediaInternational

Editor: Gwendolyn Parker and Ian McAlister

MotionMediaInternational

18 Martha Jane Ave

Killcare 2257

Table of Contents

Preface 5
Chapter 1
Challenge Is a Gift By John Spender 9
Chapter 2
Stepping Out of the Mould - The journey into my conscious way of life! By Kara Dono 33
Chapter 3
Alive and Kick'in By Linda Buller 61
Chapter 4
Lessens Embedded in Life by Scott Cohen 97
Chapter 5
Why am I here? By Michele Cempaka 117
Chapter 6
My Courageous Journey of Transformation By Julie Kennedy 135
Chapter 7
Thriving, My Way Authenticity does not always come easily By Trish Rock 159
Chapter 8
The Journey of Recovery By Alexandra Calamel 191
Chapter 9
My Journey to Spiritual Awakening By Ganga Dev 213
Author Biographies 233
Closing words 241

Preface

I created this book and chose the different experts to share their personal insights, wisdom, and experiences to assist people who may be going through challenges, adversities, or changes similar to those of the authors.

Like all of us, each author has a unique story and insight to share with you. It just may be the case that one or more of these authors have lived through an experience that is similar to your situation right now and their words are the words you need to read to help you through it. Perhaps reading about one or more of these experiences will fill in the missing piece of your puzzle, so to speak.

Storytelling has been the way humankind has communicated ideas and learning throughout our civilization. While we have become more sophisticated, and life in the modern world is more convenient, there is still much discontent and dissatisfaction with one's reality. Many people have also moved away from reading books, and they are missing out on valuable information that can help them to move forward in life with a positive outlook. I think it is important to turn off the T.V., to slow down, and to read, reflect, and take the time to appreciate everything you have in life.

I like anthology books because they carry many different perspectives and insights on a singular topic. I find that sometimes when I'm reading a book that has just one author I gain an understanding of their perspective and writing very quickly and the reading becomes predicable. With this book and all of the books in the A Journey of Riches book series, you have many different writing styles and viewpoints that will help to shape your own perspective on your current set of circumstances.

Anthology books are also great because you can start from any chapter and gain a valuable insight or a nugget of wisdom without the feeling that you have missed something from the earlier chapters.

I love reading many different types of personal development books because learning and personal growth is important to me. If you are not learning and growing, well, you're staying the same. Everything in the universe is growing, expanding, and changing. If we are not open to different ideas and different ways of thinking and being, then we can become close-minded.

The idea of this book series is to open you up to different ways of perceiving your reality, to give you hope, to give you encouragement, and to give to many avenues of thinking about the same subject. My wish for you is to feel empowered to make a decision that will best suit you in moving forward with your life. As Albert Einstein said, we cannot solve problems with the same level of thinking that created them.

With Einstein's words in mind, let your mood pick a chapter in the book and allow yourself to be guided to find the answers you seek.

Chapter 1

Challenge Is a Gift
By John Spender

It can be hard to imagine that sunshine exists when you're in the eye of a dark storm. The same can be said about finding the benefit in the challenges that you are currently faced with in your life. It's after a heavy storm that we gain a renewed appreciation for the sun and all the good it brings.

The sixth book in the *A Journey of Riches* series, *The Benefit of Challenge*, aims to highlight the gift of your current problems in the present moment through the diverse collection of stories by people from all walks of life. They will take you on a heartfelt journey into the dark tunnel through aspects of their lives and, with tips and insights, bring you back into the light of life.

In my chapter, I'm going to explore the impact that language patterns have on your current situation, as well as ways you can see the rainbow through the clouds of issues you may be facing right now. I want to show you how various inspiring people used their challenges to create their own circumstances. Because it doesn't matter where you are in life, if you are willing to fight for your idea and persist with the beat of your own drum, you will eventually bend reality with favorable outcomes.

Defining a vision for what you want and stepping into alignment with your most fulfilling values, problems start to become opportunities, and opportunities allow you to become a bigger brighter version of yourself even when your reality may seem like it's working against you. Changing the way you view and articulate your challenges will encourage you to orientate and embrace the solution mindset. The solution mindset is devoid of blame, shame, guilt, or fear. The self-talk is more like, okay, this isn't what I was expecting, but it must be leading me to an even better outcome than I anticipated, and that's a good thing. Dr. John Demartini often says, and I'm paraphrasing a little bit here: When you are congruent with your highest values, you start to see challenges merely as obstacles on the way to creating your vision, instead of in the way. And I love that insight. In *Book 4* of the series, I write about ascertaining your values, creating your perfect day, and how to make a vision board for your life. That chapter will help you gain a better understanding of what you want and why you want to create it.

Research Your Challenge

Early in 2016, when I was working on the movie documentary that I'm producing about the gift in adversity, I was lucky to be able to interview Lisa Garr about how she found the blessings in a tragic accident that almost took her life. One of the nuggets of gold that she shared—and there were many of them—was about her divine storm that lead her to living the life that she lives today. She had a mountain bike accident and hit her head, and she suffered memory lost, dizzy spells, and dramatic mood swings. Through all the pain and the not knowing if she was going to make it came the drive to do her own research about the brain and to explore possible avenues for her to live a normal life again. If you haven't heard of Lisa Garr, she hosts one of the most popular personal development radio shows in the world, *The Aware Show* and she wrote the best-selling book, *Becoming Aware: How to Repattern Your Brain and Revitalize Your Life*.

Lisa was a competitive mountain bike rider and, on this particular race at the California State Championships, she severely damaged her right pre-frontal cortex after passing out at the top of the mountain and tumbling down unconscious into a riverine at the bottom of the mountain with a destroyed helmet and heavy concussion. A helicopter airlifted her to hospital and the doctor was asking Lisa her name and basic personal information, but she didn't know how to answer.

As a result, she was unable to speak properly, and she lost a large part of her memory and became afraid of herself. After doing some research and with trial and error, she found an incredible neurofeedback specialist by the name of Dr. Barry Sternman. He helped her to discover and rebuild the neurons that were asleep and lying dormant in her brain. Talking about her experiences helped her to heal, and as part of her research, she started to interview these doctors and healers. To date, she has interviewed more than 4,000 experts. As she was interviewing these healers, she was implementing their techniques and strategies which were aiding her own healing process.

Her daily practice became about absorbing information and recreating it the next day, day in and day out. This brain exercise is how she built *The Aware Show* which has been aired on radio stations all around the world, reaching millions of people through her show and Hay House Radio. *The Aware Show* has been on air for 17 years now, and she has interviewed people like Dr. Wayne Dyer, Caroline Myss, Dr. Bruce Lipton, and many more. Lisa's experience is a perfect example of taking a negative, hopeless situation and turning it into a movement that continues to heal herself and a community of people from around the world today. This was all because she decided to research her challenges and to become empowered to share her learnings with the world. It's important to embrace our challenges and to stop looking at them or our situation as if it is a mistake or punishment of some sort. We all create our circumstances on some level, and it is a matter of taking ownership and looking for the benefit of our situation.

Letting Go Meets Patience

For the same film I was interviewing Lisa, I also wanted to feature Jack Canfield. I first heard of Jack in 2008 when I watched the hit personal development movie, *The Secret,* and later I read the first *Chicken Soup for the Soul* book, followed by the *Aladdin Factor,* again with Mark Victor Hansen and his bible, *The Success Principals*. Canfield has an inspiring story of growing up with an alcoholic father who thought that money didn't grow on trees, and his dad's favorite saying was, "Who do you think we are, the Rockefellers?" Obviously, with language patterns like that, Jack's family was poor. He is now a leading motivational speaker, author, and trainer. Jack also holds the Guinness World Record for having seven books on the *New York Times* best-seller list at the same time. He has more than 500,000 million books in print, available in 40 different languages. He is one inspiring yet humble guy.

He came from nothing and achieved so much in his life, and he continues to do so. The question I was faced with was, How do I get Jack Canfield in the film? One of the other guests in the film, Ade Djajamihardja, who is also a best-selling author and motivational speaker and good friends with Jack, put me in touch with Jack's people and the rest should have been real easy.

As it turned out, I wasn't being flexible enough with the times to meet and film Jack. I should also mention that most of Jack's staff have been with him for 10 years or more, and they are extremely protective of his time. The last message I received was, "Due to his busy schedule, Jack will have to decline his appearance in the film." Naturally I was disappointed, but Ade was in shock and phoned me from his home in Melbourne; I was already in Los Angeles filming. He couldn't believe that I had let the opportunity of filming Jack slip through my fingers. I told him that there was no point crying over spilled milk, but he sounded very disappointed with me. I then received a call from Ade's wife, and she encouraged me to call Jack's people again and offer different dates for filming. I had a feeling that the call wasn't going to go well, but I decided to call anyway.

When I made the call, I said that I was from Motion Media International. Well, the tone of Jack's head of PR was positive and enthusiastic until I told her exactly who I was and what I wanted. Her tone changed instantly. She said, "I thought I told you that Jack was busy." I apologized and explained that I was wrong to be rigid with the dates, but she wasn't having any of it and simply said that Jack won't be in the film and hung up. I just laughed to myself and thought, well that's that. We finished filming the various guests and we flew back to Bali. Six months had passed, and during this time we had filmed many guests from all over the world, including the inspiring Ade Djajamihardja at his home in Melbourne. I had booked another trip to the States to film more inspiring guests, when Ade's wife, Kate, kindly suggested that I message Jack's team again. We both agreed that enough time had passed and we had nothing to lose. Also, the list of guests that my team had filmed was pretty impressive.

Here is the email that I sent Jack's team.

Dear xyz,

I hope you are well and loving life. Kate Stephens introduced me to you earlier in February this year about Jack Canfield appearing in the new film I'm producing about discovering the richness in adversity featuring Rev. Michael Bernard Beckwith,

Dr John F Demartini and Jack's good friend Ade Djajamihardja and many more.

I'll be back in the States with my crew from September the 10th to the 5th of October filming various big names in personal development and we would love to feature Jack in the film. We would only need 30minutes of Jack's time and we can come to you guys to make things easier. We are also flexible with dates and can come at a date and time that suits Jack best.

Looking forward to your response.

Kind Regards

John

Lucky for me, Jack reconsidered his involvement in the movie and we filmed him in his lounge room. I remember being nervous when we arrived but projecting outward confidence, and I remember not wanting to flatter him too much. It was one of the most memorable experiences of my filming adventure and I really appreciate Jack's generosity with his time. He also gave all the crew a copy of his updated limited edition of *The Success Principals*. This highlighted for me the benefit of letting time pass after the initial rejection and letting go of the disappointment quickly. I simply focused on raising money for the film and landing interviews with inspiring guests from around the world. Patience was also a key factor and making adjustments from my first approach.

Adversity Leads to a Billion Dollars

I was recently surfing YouTube when I came across the Airbnb story. After watching it, I was amazed at how the founders, Brian Chesky and Joe Gebbia, took their down-and-out situation and made it into a billion-dollar company. They had found themselves in San Francisco in an apartment they couldn't afford to stay in. After brain storming, and inspired by an international design conference that was in town, they decided to take some air mattresses, put them on the floor of their apartment, and charge people to stay over. And Air Beds and Breakfasts began. They were expecting to attract university students that didn't have much money, but they were wrong; they had three people stay with them—all over the age of 30 and all wanting to attend this conference. That was the beginning of what we know today as Airbnb. Of course, they were faced with many challenges along the way. In the beginning, people were saying that it was the worst idea to ever work, and many other people were saying it was the worst idea ever. From the first 20 angel investors that they emailed, not one of them said yes. One particular investor, whom they met in a café, left half-way through their pitch and didn't even finish his smoothie. No one wanted to touch their idea.

The two friends from design school were the only ones who believed in their idea, so much so that they had a binder that you would ordinarily use for baseball cards; however, they put all their credit cards in the sleeves and they had to convince themselves daily that everything was going to work out. It was around about this time, inundated with credit card debit, that they found out about couch surfing. But couch surfing was free! Where there is a will there is a way. This was back in 2008 during President Obama's Presidential campaign. The Democratic National Convention in Denver, Colorado, was having one of its rallies for Obama, and they moved it into an 80,000-seat football stadium. News stations were blowing the story up, saying there was a major accommodation shortage. The boys saw their opportunity, having now been joined by Nate Blecharczyk, a Harvard graduate with a bachelor's degree in computer science.

After many failed attempts to contact various news stations, the partners decided to contact small bloggers and ask them to write about their Airbnb solution. Then they asked medium successful bloggers and found that bloggers were already writing about them. They agreed. Of course, the next step was to email large bloggers, and they saw that many bloggers were writing about them and they published their story as well. They then got the *Denver Post* and the *Rocky Mountain News* to write pieces. Then they got on the local *NBC News*, and they started getting all this press, including the *New York Times* and *CNN News*.

They had 50 people in the Colorado area ready with air mattresses to accommodate guests, and they ended up having 80 people to stay in Denver. But even after all the publicity and web traffic, people were still not catching on to the idea. Their main drivers for business were these conventions, but they weren't on every weekend, and people were still saying this was the worst idea ever. The guys had built a market place, but no one was really using it except at the Democratic National Conventions which were touring around the country. So, after brain storming in their kitchen, Brian and Joe, who were still living together and had a lot of time on their hands, and their new partner, Nate, came up with an idea of sending breakfast cereal to the various hosts.

They came up with Obama O's and the slogan, "Hope in Every Bowl." They designed the boxes and hot glued them together, but they didn't have cereal to put into the boxes. At this point, they had almost maxed out all of their credit cards. They made Obama and John McCain themed cereal boxes and promotional videos with quirky jingles. The John McCain cereal was called Cap'n McCain's, after the fact that he used to be a captain in the U.S. Navy. The McCain cereal also came with its own promotional video and jingle as well. The idea was, if they could sell 100,000 boxes of the Presidential election candidates' cereal at two dollars each, they could raise $200,000 dollars in capital and fund their company. The problem was that Brian and Joe were about 15-20 grand in credit card debt each. They ended up meeting an old friend from their days at college who offered to lend them enough money to print 1,000 cereal boxes: 500 John McCain boxes and 500 Barak Obama boxes. To make enough money, they had to charge a lot more than two dollars a box. So, they marketed the cereal as "limited edition" and charged $40 a box. Remember, they still needed the cereal, and so they went to various stores in the suburbs and in the ghettos where they could buy cereal for a dollar, and they bought a thousand boxes of cereal for a dollar each.

They ended up stuffing the dollar cereal into the presidential boxes and sent them to the press, and they received a ton of media exposure. In about three days they sold out of all of the Obama O's. They didn't sell many of the Cap'n McCain's, but people were reselling the Obama O's on Craig's List and e-Bay from $70 to $500 dollars a box.

The team raised enough money to settle their debts, but not much was left over and they literally lived off the Cap'n McCain's cereal for three weeks until they had their lucky break. They applied for funding with Y Combinator which is a start-up incubator based in Mountain View, CA, in Silicon Valley. Co-founder, Nate, had moved to Boston to get married, and their future as a trio and start-up company wasn't looking great. Nate needed to fly back to San Francisco for their funding interview with Y Combinator co-founder, Paul Graham. This was the last chance for the trio and Airbnb as a company. Apparently, Paul Graham couldn't believe that people were actually renting out blow up mattresses and thought that something must be wrong with them. The interview wasn't going well, and the trio was asked to leave, but Joe took two boxes of the Presidential cereals and gave them to Paul Graham, then told him the whole story of how they had sold this cereal. Paul was amazed at their resilience and gave them $20,000, accepting the company into the Y Combinator's seed funding program.

Even though Paul Graham thought it was a crazy idea, he reasoned that if they could convince people to pay $40 for a $4 box of breakfast cereal, then they could probably convince people to pay money to sleep on air beds. This was the very beginning of Airbnb, and they now have over 3,000,000 listings in 65,000 cities in over 180 countries. And they don't own any of the listings; they simply receive a brokerage fee. That's what is possible when you see challenges as a necessary process for fulfilling your idea and vision. In March of 2017, Airbnb raised $1 billion in additional funding, bringing their total funding to date to more than $3 billion, valuing the company at $31 billion. That's what you call a success story born out of challenge. It blows my mind to think that all of this started with an air bed in a lounge room so two college friends could pay the rent.

The Power of Imagination

The idea came to JK Rowling while she was traveling on a train from Manchester to London in 1990. Only nine years later, the first three *Harry Potter* books—*Harry Potter and the Sorcerer's Stone*, *Harry Potter and the Chamber of Secrets,* and *Harry Potter and the Prisoner of Azkaban*-- had earned approximately $480 million in only three years, with over 35 million copies in print in 35 languages. The idea came to her very clearly, and she wasn't even thinking about writing. She could see this scrawny little boy as clear as day, and she had a physical rush of excitement, nothing like she had ever experienced before in her life, as she mentions in an interview. She had all of these ideas jumbling around in her head and no pen or paper to write them on. As soon as she arrived back in her apartment, Harry was born and she wrote about him for some 17 years.

The first book took five years to write and she made 15 attempts at writing the first chapter because she found herself revealing too much of the plot. Rowling spent much time sketching the various characters to get a sense of who they were. The Harry books were born out of depression when Rowling lost her mom, Anne, aged 45, after ten years of suffering from multiple sclerosis. Rowling was writing *Harry Potter* during the end of her mother's illness and had never told her about it. After three years in Portugal teaching English and divorcing the father of her young daughter, Rowling found herself back in Edinburgh with very little money and no job. She had to write on napkins to begin with because she couldn't afford paper. She was 28 and living on social benefits, which was about $70 a week, and she couldn't afford child care to work even if she'd wanted to. She used to write in cafes because her baby daughter, Jessica, would fall asleep while Rowling pushed her along in the stroller, and once she fell asleep, the young mother would go into the nearest cafe and write. The owner was her brother-in-law, who tolerated her taking up a table and not really ordering anything. Rock bottom became the foundation on which she built her life, and she used failure to create her success.

Her belief in the story is what kept her going, even when she knew that it would be difficult for an unknown author to get published. She sent her manuscript to her agent, who told her that the book was going to be challenging to sell. Most of the publishers were saying that it was too long for a children's book. Her agent told her that he really liked the book, but it just wasn't commercial enough and she had best keep her job. She eventually became published by Bloomsbury Publishing after 12 major publishers had rejected her manuscript, and she received about four thousand dollars. Of course, it wasn't just about the money; Rowling was so excited to finally be in print. Yet, the deal meant she didn't have to live hand-to-mouth anymore.

Her real name is Joanne Rowling, but her publisher thought that the book would most likely appeal to boys, and they didn't want the boys to know that a woman had written it. They asked her to allow them to use her initials instead of her name, but she only had one initial, as she had no middle name at all. So, she used her favorite grandmother's name, Kathleen. Thus, the birth of JK Rowling was complete.

Rowling was still working as a teacher in Edinburgh when American publishers were caught in a bidding war for the rights to the first book in the States. Scholastic Publishing won the rights and paid an advance of $105,000—more money they had given any previous author, let alone one for a first novel. That was in 1997. This meant that JK Rowling could finally fulfill her lifetime ambition of being a full-time writer. In 1999, her third book was released. With *Harry Potter and the Prisoner of Azkaban,* Rowling became a rock star. Her book signings in the U.S. were more like rock concerts than book signings, with queues of people, fancy dress costumes, and fans screaming with excitement. In Toronto, 12,000 people attended the biggest book reading ever recorded. I watched footage of that reading, and when JK Rowling was introduced, it sounded like a huge rock concert. It was so loud that Rowling had to use ear plugs. She went from complete obscurity to suddenly being famous, all in a blink of an eye.

Jo Rowling had always wanted to be a writer, but if it hadn't been for her failed marriage in Portugal and finding herself back home with no money, she may have never written the *Harry Potter* book series and might not have become one of the biggest contributors to increasing child literacy around the world. She is also the first author to become a billionaire as the seventh book in the series, *Harry Potter and the Deathly Hallows,* sold more than 8.3 million copies within the first 24 hours, making it the fastest selling book in history to date.

The power of belief is a strange thing, even when our physical reality is telling us that there is no way out. Living on welfare and struggling in life could have been the way it was going to be for Jo Rowling, but she believed in her book when no one else did.

In all the cases that I shared, the underlying thread that I see is one of focusing on the value, solving a problem, and giving first without knowing if you will get anything back in return. Along with character traits of perseverance, determination, and trusting your intuition, all are key ingredients to a winning mindset and knowing the outcome that you desire, even if it is to just start-up company like the Airbnb boys or to become a published writer like Jo Rowling. Start with what you would like to do rather than what is safe and secure. It's generally the risky and scary option, but—hey—regret feels worse.

Quite often when I travel to different countries, I like to visit graveyards and read the various tombstones. I imagine what the lives of the deceased might have been like in the era in which they grew up and lived out their lives. I wonder about their quality of life and whether or not they'd lived fully. I ask myself how many of the people buried here died with their dreams unfulfilled, and I look out into the sea of tombstones. This little ritual fills me with determination and spirit for the journey ahead, and it reminds me to enjoy the privilege of being alive. Too many of the graves are of people who died too young.

Watch Your Language

Challenges are there to expand our capabilities and to determine what is possible for our lives, to forge the character needed to create the desired end results. Sometimes that means sitting with the tension of doing nothing, while other times it means being consistently productive. And sometimes massive action is required. Having the flexibility and the intuition to know when to do which course of action or non-action naturally takes practice and the willingness to make mistakes and move on quickly. What I notice and work on with my coaching clients is their language patterns. What we think and speak about, we bring into our reality. All of your current reality is the sum of your past thinking, feeling, and doing patterns, which means you can change your reality because all we really have is right now.

A couple of ways to change your reality is through self-awareness and changing your language patterns. The words that we speak have an invoking power that helps to shape our experiences. If you speak about things that you don't want, then—guess what—the chances of you getting what you don't want will increase. For example, if you are walking around saying, "I don't want to kick my toe," you can guess what is going to happen, right? Of course, you're going to kick your toe. What we focus on expands, and our creating facility, the sub conscious mind, doesn't hear the negative words. For instance, when using disempowering phrases like "don't drop It," all the brain computes is "drop it." Alternatively, one could say, "catch it." Another disempowering language pattern to watch for is "Don't forget." Rather, try saying, "Remember to get the milk." "I can't" is yet another disempowering language pattern. Disempowering words are sneaky and quite often go undetected, sometimes for a lifetime.

Earlier this year, I went to my friend's Brazilian Jiu Jitsu instructor's house here in Bali to increase my fitness and to see what all the fuss was about, because my friend had been raving about it. The class was small and most of the students were first-timers, which made things easier. We were taught various moves, and then we practiced with each other. This was a little awkward, as none of us knew what we were doing. The drills and exercises became more intense as the class went on, making self-control challenging as we naturally began to get tired. I wrestled with two friends and I dominated them, only because I was bigger. The instructor saw this and immediately wanted to have ago with me. I said, "I can't." I never even realized that I said it until he pulled me up and said, "Of course you can."

When you are in the moment, it is very easy to be unaware of your language and how self-defeating your words can be to your own detriment. One technique you can use is to celebrate every time that you catch yourself using self-defeating language. I do a little fist pump, with my right fist and I replace the negative statement with a positive affirmation. This includes self-talk and thoughts that we think. For example, instead of "It's hard to get my clients to pay on time," catch yourself and then celebrate with a "Yes!" and a right-hand fist pump. Replace the negative with a positive affirmation like "Money comes to me easily and frequently." It sounds easy enough to do, and it can be with consistency. Give it a go and see how many times you can catch yourself during the day.

Catching your language early helps you to stay in peak mental state. To aid this, I recommend meditation, taking regular breaks throughout the day, and exercise to keep the mind fresh. Tony Robbins has been known to use a mini trampoline jumping on it throughout the day. The rebounding movements of jumping up and down exercise a huge range of the body's muscles and exercises the thousands of one-way lymph valves and ducts in the body. This helps with the body's circulation and fitness while increasing one's overall mood when used throughout the day on a consistent basis. Plus, there are other benefits, like muscle tone and back pain relief.

You can even say affirmations while you use the rebounder. Affirmations really do work, especially when you use them throughout the day. A good friend of mine, Casey Plouffe, was a nurse before she became a network marketing seven-figure earner. One of the keys to her outrageous success was her strong mindset game. She would read a book a week, sometimes the same book week after week. She joined group calls, attended retreats, listened to audios in her car, and she had affirmations throughout her house. Her three favorite places are called the three S's: the shower, the shitter (toilet), and the sheets (bedroom). I never saw the ones in her bedroom, but the ones in the bathroom are glued to the back of the door, and she has a laminated sheet on a shelf inside the shower. I was amazed at her level of commitment in keeping her mindset fortified. At first, she used to borrow affirmations that she'd read in books from other people. After a while, she developed her own affirmations based on situations or circumstances that she wanted to create in her life. One experience that she shared of her tailor-made affirmations was when she used to say, "I have more leads for my business than time." Sure enough, that's exactly what happened, and naturally that wasn't a lot of fun after a while. And, so, she changed it to "People show up in my business and produce with or without me." That was a much better one for her. I challenge you to come up with 10 affirmations that you can say to yourself throughout the day and start invoking your desired reality into existence.

I hope my chapter has helped you to shift the way that you see challenges in your life and to realize that adversity is one of the best catalysts to propel you forward towards your desired reality and lifestyle. Use challenge and hardship to stay true to your tune and watch doors open out of nowhere and no way.

Chapter 2

Stepping Out of the Mould - The journey into my conscious way of life!
By Kara Dono

Born into the normal way of life

We come into this world as conscious and spiritual souls. We bring our past lives from the spiritual paradigm and enter a new life through our chosen parents. It's all a conscious journey - full of life lessons and experiences. I came into the world as an extremely shy, sensitive and introverted soul in the land of the long white cloud in New Zealand.

I loved my own time and playing and creating by myself. I was a dreamer, caught up in my own imaginary world. I would spend hours as a child watching nature and meaningful observations of sacred mother earth. I was curious by nature and enjoyed the simple pleasures of life, for example; one day when I was only 5 years old and I remember sitting for hours watching the water evaporate from a beautiful heart shaped rock. These experiences felt like where I belonged. It was a calm and meditative type of state.

I suppressed my intuitive gift

Though outside of nature and these fond meditative experiences was the stress and chaos of life. Family and friends just looked at me as this extremely shy child. I pulled myself inside because I could hear what others were thinking. As a child I didn't realise this was a special gift. I went on to suppress this gift, as the clutter of my inside voice was too much for my innocent ears.

Going through the motions of life

Primary school, high school and university years went by and life was fine because I always had my dear friend Sally by my side to speak up for me and guide me on my way. In my last year of high school I met the love of my life, Simon (name changed for confidentiality). I was curious with Simon because he was wild, crazy and free spirited. He was the opposite of my very routine and normal family upbringing. He introduced me to the nightclub scene and was a social soul. Life was easy with Simon. There was always a fun party and lots of friends around. I loved spending time with his Latino family because they always were celebrating life with music, food and laughs.

Simon encouraged me to follow a passion and career, so I became a primary school teacher. This helped my introverted personality to become more extroverted, expressive and confident. I had a passion for working with children and watching them learn and shine.

Manifesting a new reality

Simon was my rock and we went on to get married and have two adorable sons.

I remember daydreaming whilst breastfeeding my youngest son thinking I would love to experience living on a tropical island with my sons. One day a spiritual friend, named Genevieve, said to me. "Kara you were in my dream last night". "Really," I said… "what happened in the dream?" She said, "I saw you talking to an angel and expressing your desire for freedom, change and adventure; you were surrounded by this purple light". This conversation was so intriguing and liberating. I suddenly felt hope and lightness. She went on to tell me that I have a manifestation gift and I should give it a go.

I was extremely skeptical and wasn't normally open to the mysteries of life. I reflected upon Genevieve's words when I went home that day and put my sons to bed for their midday sleep after reading a story and giving them a heartfelt hug. I sat down to a cup of tea and imagined myself living freely and simply on a tropical island. It felt like a different reality and realm. This was like a new meditation for me; this fantasyland brought some kind of hope to my monotonous rut life that I was living.

One month later my family and I were on a holiday in Darwin when Simon got a phone call from a friend in Jakarta saying there is a job waiting for him in Indonesia, and to get himself and his family to Indonesia as soon as possible. I was so excited, thrilled and also nervous. Wow, I thought, I have never lived overseas before. Will I enjoy this experience? I became resistant as I thought about the friends I would be leaving behind. Did I help to create this with my daily manifestation? I felt overwhelming confused. We decided to set the family up in Bali and Simon did fly in and fly out, working in Kalimantan.

First taste of living abroad

My 3 and 4 year old sons instantly adjusted to life in Bali. They were free spirited souls on the beach and were fascinated by the ceremonies and offerings of daily life.

Life suddenly became richer. There seemed to be more purpose and excitement in life. I was living and socialising with people from all walks of life - different religions, cultures and countries, though we all came together in unity. The Balinese were so welcoming and patiently explained the meaning behind the rituals and ceremonies. I was fascinated by the way they openly shared and talked about life and death as the cycle of life. I felt this loving and gentle feminine energy amongst the people and my soul felt safe and nurtured.

Every day I woke with overwhelming gratitude. I would often pinch myself to remind myself that it wasn't just a dream. I was living this abundant life full of freedom, ritual, purpose and balance. Sometimes I asked myself, do I deserve this? I must be one of the most fortunate people in the world. Simon organised security, drivers, and maids to support me at home. I had a new love and respect for Simon; working hard to provide this lifestyle for his family. Putu, my maid, and Wayan, my driver, embraced my sons and they became our Bali family.

Taking the red matrix pill

Life was perfect in its own amazing way. My dear shamanic/healing friend Michele Cempaka contacted me one day to tell me about a transformational 2-day workshop she was attending and invited me along. "Sure" I said, I was always interested in learning and new opportunities, even though I was extremely skeptical.

The facilitator told us that many people actually regret doing this workshop because they see beyond the illusion of life and the truth is revealed. I thought she was nuts! What could possibly change in my life I said! I doubted this workshop even more and wondered why I was even attending! The facilitator went on to explain it's like the Matrix movie, you can take the red pill or the blue pill! "You take the **blue pill**, the story ends. You wake up in your bed and believe whatever you want to believe. You take the **red pill**, you stay in Wonderland, and I show you how deep the rabbit hole goes." The term red pill refers to a human that is aware of the true nature of the **Matrix**. So this is where my true awakening and transformation began…..

Of course we didn't take a pill, though the transformational journey opened us up in unexpected ways.

The start of the rabbit hole - my life came
at a high price

Two weeks later I was celebrating Father's Day with Simon. He requested to play golf for Father's Day and asked me to come along. After, my parents came to join us for lunch with our sons. We were all sitting around enjoying Indonesian cuisine and participating in small talk. I picked up Simon's phone to check the time and I felt an instant sinking feeling in my heart as I read several explicit messages from other women. I had this sudden urgency to get home. I held back all my tears and emotions, stood up and said we need to leave.

Simon looked at me confused. "What's wrong? What happened? Did you see something on my phone?" I couldn't hear anything, it was like the whole world fell silent. I felt like a little girl that just wanted to numb out the world by not listening. As Wayan, the driver, pulled into our garage I jumped out of the car then sat outside on the hammock and felt my head spin around.

The facilitator was right I thought. It feels like I have taken a pill from the Matrix and all the lies, secrets and betrayals are being revealed! The truth is being exposed! How did I have no idea? Just like the facilitator said, "your true life will be revealed to you…." and 2 weeks to the day my life was smashed in my face. My high life came at a high price!

I stood up from the hammock and walked outside. I didn't feel like I belonged in my own home. I felt disconnected-alone-scared. My body began to feel numb and I collapsed to the ground and had a shock attack. In the moment my heart fell into a million pieces. Wayan came running to me "Kara, Kara, what's wrong with you? Should I take you to the hospital? Is it the food? I think you have food poisoning". With his strong solid frame over my curled up body he picked me up in his arms and carried me inside to my bed. He gently placed me down and worryingly looked at Simon and said "Kara needs some help. She is so weak and limp and is very pale". Then he left the room. Simon looked down to the floor in disgrace and guilt. The secret was out… the double life… the lies….the adultery.

I got up from the bed and walked outside. I felt so alienated from my home. I didn't feel like I belonged in the family we had created. I felt like running away with the little strength I had. I had glimpses of Tom Hanks in the Forest Gump movie running and running. Maybe I will just run out of Bali… where will I go? Where do I belong? I never had felt so rejected, lonely, scared and hopeless in my life. Wayan kept carrying me to the bed and Simon kept watching me walk out. He was also numb and scared. Then I stood up with overwhelming rage and furry! What were you thinking? I grabbed his mobile and threw it across the room. I watched his expensive Blackberry mobile bounce off the wall. He saw the turmoil in my eyes and started protecting himself with his arms like a little child. The anger that rose from this weak body was enough to smash down a wall. I felt like a scorned woman.

Simon got up and said "I have a plane to catch, I need to get to Surabaya". I got a taxi to a friend's house and politely asked the maid to stay with the boys. My friend Nelly lived at a five star hotel. Like many expats, her husband worked in the hotel industry. She took one look at me and knew something bad had happened. I sat on her couch for hours talking numbly.

I regretted my life.

I regretted knowing.

I regretted finding out the truth because it was too painful.

I regretted doing the transformational course because my life was suddenly smashed against my face.

The breakdown

Days and months that followed felt so dark and empty. I felt stuck down in the rabbit hole not knowing how to crawl out. I spent days crying, yelling and hitting my pillow. I abandoned the house duties and asked darling Putu to step in and do all the shopping and organise everything. I was too sad and empty to parent. I felt so emotionally drained.

Simon revealed everything. The 5 years of infidelity. His sex addiction, black magic and the power/control he felt over women. It was as though I suddenly saw another side of Simon. A side I never saw in the 16 years we were together.

The story going around and around in my head was exhausting. Was it him? Was it me? Why couldn't he talk to me? I had never withheld sex? Why wasn't I enough? How can you live and marry someone and not fully know who they are? I loved Simon unconditionally and followed him and his career. Was I not good enough in bed? Did I give too much time and love to our sons and not enough to my husband?

I felt like I was going crazy. My mind was going in overdrive. I struggled to sleep and some days dragged myself out of bed to take the boys to school, though most days I sent them with Wayan. He understood my suffering and gave me space to rest.

My girlfriend Nelly came over to see me one day and explained that prostitutes wear no condoms in Indonesia as they get more money that way! I was so angry… Simon wouldn't put me at risk of contracting HIV! After all, I'm the mother of his sons. A call to Simon confirmed that I needed to be tested because he only had unprotected sex! I yelled into the phone about how selfish he was and hung up. So my girlfriend drove me to the clinic for testing and then 3 months later we did the follow up testing. Thankfully it all came back negative though I was left with the question "What if…". Who would be the mum of my sons if I was HIV positive? Who would be there to support me through the sickness? How can I trust again? The person I called my husband and shared my biggest secrets with in life was suddenly my enemy.

I started to hate my body. I felt disgusting and ugly. I felt like I wasn't good enough. My body wasn't good enough, that's why he was searching for something else, I told myself. I was creating these stories in my head. I was questioning and analysing everything.

Simon came clean and told me the stories of black magic being put on him in Surabaya, the prostitutes all over Indonesia and the exclusive brothel that was on our own street! We had deep and meaningful conversations about life, trauma, addictions and sex. For the first time, I discovered that he viewed masturbation as 'naughty, dirty and evil'. This was the beginning of my learning and fascination into sex. I delved deep into patterning, beliefs and thoughts around sex, the porn industry, prostitution, Tantra, Taoist sexual practices and Karma Sutra.

Finding happiness through the external world

I started searching externally for comfort; enjoying fancy holidays, fancy beach clubs and extravagant resorts. Simon was over indulgent with his money and with me he was very generous and giving as it helped ease some of his guiltiness. He would do anything to put a fake smile on my face. He constantly asked me to forgive him, move on and create a new life. He was asking me to leave the shocking past and pretend it never happened, like burying the betrayal in the sand. It may have been that simple for him, though it seemed impossible for me. How could I trust him? How could I love someone that hurt me so badly? I just asked him for time and space.

Part of me felt like I was mourning the death of our marriage. Part of me wanted to walk out on the marriage, though I was too afraid. Where would I move? How would I be a single parent to my 4 and 5 year old sons? How would I financially cope? I was in love with Bali and the lifestyle, so I talked myself into staying in the marriage and craved the high life!

I learnt self-coping skills and how to pretend to be happy. My mask would cover up my inner sadness, especially at my son's international school which helped stop all the gossip and rumours. A few friends judged me for staying in the marriage.

Life just felt like one confusing mess. I felt like I was meant to be in Bali when this secret was revealed. I couldn't help but wonder how I would have dealt with the situation if I was living in the Western world? Would I suppress most of my emotions, pick myself up and just get on with it? Would these suppressed emotions go on to cause sickness in my body? Would I just be arguing with Simon all the time and walk out on the marriage there and then?

The Awakening

All I knew was that this was the beginning of my awakening. I had been smashed against the wall and I began to peel off each part of my fragmented soul and self heal. I became obsessed with reading self development books, meditating, seeing healers, shamans, breath work, doing yoga and all that I could fit into a school day. I wanted to feel better, I wanted to get better, and so my self-sabbatical had begun. I was constantly searching for answers in my nurturing, healing home.

Bali attracted healers from all over the World. The creative, feminine and gentle energy was a paradise for energetic releases and transformational work. Every year I excitedly participated in the annual Bali Spirit Festival. Between the vegan delights, healing hut and stages for yoga, breath work, workshops, classes, ecstatic dance and shows, there was so much to juice up the soul. Also opportunities to chill out in a hammock or lie next to the pool looking onto the rainforest or explore water shiatsu.

I was drawn towards an international healer named Alison Levesley from England. I booked in for a 1 hour session and as she worked through my chakras, clearing out blockages, I burst into tears. She helped to release stagnant energy in my sacral chakra and explained to me this is the chakra for creativity and sexual healing. The anger of the infidelity was hurting my lower stomach area. She helped me to forgive Simon. She told me I was living too much in my head and I needed to let go of the clutter and the stories that were holding me back and make space for new creations in my life.

Living after forgiveness

I went on to forgive Simon for the infidelity, though I felt empty and stuck. I was clearly in the marriage for financial freedom, lifestyle and the children - though that's not the story I was telling myself! I was telling myself a lie, it seemed easier and more comfortable.

I continued working monthly with Alison. She could see that I was living for Simon and my sons and not my own desires so she encouraged me to go back to my career. That morning as I turned on my computer I read about Green School needing a Primary School Teacher. That is a sign I thought, so I prepared my resume and made contact with the school and they invited me in for an interview.

The bamboo structured International school was so impressive to the eye. Situated in the jungle with beautiful views and yoga studios, the school was a dream. They had 'wall-less education', so there were no doors, corners or walls. Allowing the energy to flow and the animals would also freely wander around the school. Everything was interconnected. The children would eat together in the heart of school, often eating freshly picked food from the garden. It certainly had a relaxed vibe!

I began working a few months later and instantly felt more purpose, motivation and empowerment. I remember thinking maybe I can keep living in Bali with my sons and be a single mother. I learnt so much at Green School and I was equipped to apply this to my personal life along with an educational setting. I was fascinated about the science of the brain and the benefits of taking 3 deep breaths to settle our amygdala during emotional stress. I got trained in the MindUP curriculum and felt at home starting every morning with 15 minutes of mindfulness with my class. Some days it was mindful gardening, other days it was meditating around the large school healing crystal, other days mindful movement or partner yoga.

Alternative Healing- looking at the spiritual energetic body

One day at work it was time for the class to go to Indonesian lesson, so they went off to another class. I was checking work emails when one of the students came running back breathless. Luther was from Switzerland and had broken English. I calmly asked him to take three deep tummy breaths then I lied him down to create a sense of calmness for him. He was very anxious and explained that he became emotional when asked to talk about his family during Indonesian class. I placed my hands on his forehead and suddenly was overwhelmed with the spirit of a young boy.

Luther told me he didn't want to talk about his family during Indonesian class because it brought sad memories of when his little brother died in his sleep, the funeral and the sadness it caused the family. I felt empathy for Luther and told him that his little brother is currently with us and he wants to tell you that your artwork is very talented and that every time you draw he is with you. Luther sat up with instant peace and said "really….my brother is with me when I do my artwork! No wonder I feel so calm and happy when I draw and I love it so much…".

That day, every time Luther was drawing he would make eye contact with me and smile with a strong glimpse of happiness. He knew his little brother was with him.

That day was so life changing for me…. "I've found my calling" I thought. In that moment I saw the importance of considering the spiritual needs of a child. I also discovered my suppressed psychic and intuitive gift in that moment.

The universe had other plans for me

I finished my contract at Green School and felt this calling for me to work with people using my newly found intuitive and psychic gifts. I felt like a light switch had been turned on in my cells and I found my passion and purpose in life. Suddenly life seemed to flow with ease, joy and synchronicity. I was constantly having dreams, and messages would come through during the day and I slowly learnt to trust that inner voice and surrender to the flow of life. My deceased grandma would also often come to me from the soul world.

One day a beautiful lady, named Salini, came to my villa in Bali. She was looking for a place to stay and I invited her into my guest room. We sat, had a cuppa and she explained that she was a Reiki Master and that she had strong lineage because Reiki

Grandmaster Takata lived in her family home for many years and taught her and her mother. We discussed doing a trade; I became her Reiki Master student and she stayed at my place. Every day for the next 3 months we did daily meditation and Reiki. She suggested that I invite parents from my son's international school for practice sessions, which happened daily. I was so excited because I was becoming more and more psychic with more and more practice. The visions, messages and flow of energy from my hands when I connected into the auric field were powerful. As Salini gave me more Reiki attunements I was living with more power and synchronicity.

Anne Marie

I believe people come into your life for a time or a reason and this was the case with my now dear friend Anne Marie. She is an energy healer and powerfully works with the core beliefs and patterns that can hold us back. I had several sessions with her around my self-talk, self-love and self-esteem and was often crying after the sessions as I allowed my body to recalibrate to the energy shifts. Anne Marie healed herself of breast cancer through working with the spiritual and emotional body.

Game Changer

Many friends started to feel this lightness and glow with my energy and often commented on the change. I knew the healing work with Anne Marie was life changing. I felt like I was guided and supported on a spiritual plain and the synchronicity of life allowed everything to align. Life just seemed to be easier. I felt like suddenly there weren't constant road blocks and forced control, rather everything just seemed to fall into place in a gentle surrendering motion.

The universe connected me with a strong and powerful lightworker named Bascha Meir. She did amazing shifts on me and suggested I start following a Maori shaman living in Bali named Henare O'Brien. I started reading his fascinating daily posts and watched his weekly videos. This guy is a whole next level I thought. He mentioned in a post that he was running a transformational Game Changer retreat here in Bali. I blindly signed up and next thing I know I was in a room with 60 strangers for the next 5 days from 9am-9pm.

Henare did his shamanic work and opened the portals of everyone and connected them to their highest self. Everyone was going through their own massive shifts and in the room I saw people faint, sweat, yell, dance, go crazy. Henare had a bird cage on one of the seats and explained to the audience about how most of us live our lives inside the bird cage, being safe and in a comfort zone and not willing to get out of the bird cage and be authentic and live true to ourselves or show who we really are. It was a great analogy for us all to create life on our terms and take responsibility for who we are and what we stand for. Not stuck in the vibration of fear, guilt, shame. Or living our life to please others.

On the third day I felt this shift within my cells. I faced my insecure shadow and realised that I had been pretending to be happily married and really I was craving more in life. I had been living a lie. Pretending the marriage would fix itself and everything would be okay one day. I was stuck in the story that things will get better, even though Simon and I would always fight and our friends and family could clearly see that the marriage was already hanging by a thin thread. I was stuck in this comfort zone because it kind of felt safe! Though I just knew we had grown apart and were no longer aligned.

We were all working in small groups and Henare was walking around challenging people. He had this way of shaking things up! Henare challenged me by suggesting we wrestle. He literally pushed me to the ground, pinned me down and said, "Get out". I laughed at him and then sunk into this masculine energy and this wildfire within me arose. He received a sore shoulder and was proud of my inner strength as he watched me fight to get out. He explained to me that he was guided to wrestle me to the ground to show me my strength. He told me to stop playing the weak victim game in life and to really trust my strength and to step into my power. He said "you have this inner fight and strength".

That's what it took for me to be pushed to the next level of my life. For the first time in my life I felt like a strong empowered woman. That was the moment I knew I had power and strength and that I would cope as a single mother and the bumps of life.

Uncomfortable conversation

I told many friends about my experience and that I was confident to leap into the next stage of my life. When Simon returned from working in Africa I had the uncomfortable conversation and told him I wanted to leave the marriage. He naturally didn't believe that I would take the next step. He was accustomed to the weak, disempowered and subservient wife. Suddenly it felt like a masculine and feminine power game. He suggested he would buy me like I was an object for sale and he could control me with his high salary. He said I could have whatever I wanted in life!

For me as a spiritual soul, this wouldn't fulfill my heart and desires. I wanted truth, honestly, deep communication, equality and respect. He said "I look at you like you're my property, you belong to me". I went to sleep that night and in my dream I got told that if I stayed in the marriage, my body would speak the truth and that I would eventually get very sick! I woke up with confirmation. After having the uncomfortable conversation, I instantly felt more energy and vitality for life because I was living according to my true self.

New home, new country, new career and newly separated all at once!

I went through the healing and decluttering process of clearing out my Bali home, said farewell to my Bali family and moved to Perth, Australia. I set up a new home with my sons and began seeing clients for intuitive healing and Reiki. I found new spiritual friends and attracted many beautiful souls with a similar frequency into my life. We would connect in circles for ritual, meditations and full moon manifestations.

Living with no regrets

For me, I have no regrets. I am actually so grateful for the emotional and challenging times in my life because this has been a major catalyst for growth. We learn that our challenges become our biggest assets. This is where we can step out of the mould, the norm, the society and ancestral beliefs that often hold us back in life. We can create our own lives and pave out how we want it to look. I told Simon, I take equal responsibility for the marriage breakdown and look at him with love and compassion. He is an amazing father to our sons and I respect his own journey in life.

I feel we all come into each other's lives for a time and a reason. All the lessons I have learnt over the years have enriched my life in so many ways and I am forever grateful. Sometimes I feel that I have stepped out of the matrix and social conditioning of life and live according to my own desires and dreams. I make empowered and conscious choices from my heart. I often meditate on a question or do muscle testing and allow the answers to flow to me. I feel so alive to breathe into my cells and intuitive life. I have stepped beyond the time, money and fear that was holding me back.

New Mindset- linked to our vibrational frequency

With my new life came my new mindset. All the lower vibrational frequency energies of fear, guilt, anger, sadness and shame just seemed to disappear and I felt higher vibe energies of love and joy. I was overwhelmed with feelings of freedom because I was making my own empowered choices and living my true self. I no longer was lying to myself or others and all those exhausting background stories had drifted away and I had a sense of clarity. Through doing my inner work and keeping my cup full, this has enabled me to hold space for others and support other souls on their personal journeys. I believe self-healing and inner work is a constant journey until the day we die. I learnt a lot about life through Simon, so I'm forever grateful for the overseas experiences and also seeing the dark because it has helped me work with the light. I consciously choose the food I put into my sacred temple and the music I listen to as this also affects my own resonance.

Reinvent yourself

Looking back to how I was as a child and who I am now is almost like a reinvention of the soul. James Altucher wrote the inspiring book "Reinvent Yourself'. He talks about how we have the choice to reinvent ourselves everyday by starting out with small changes in our lives to create motion and little pivoting adjustments. Accepting and allowing changes opens us up to growth and new possibilities. He said if we live our entire lives in the same job, house, country then how do we keep the motion going in life? He suggests constant reading, learning and travelling to revitalise the soul. A few steps he suggests for reinvention are:

1. Say 'no' to what doesn't serve you, so you can say 'yes' to what is really a 'fuck yes'.

2. Re-examine relationships. Set boundaries around toxic relationships.

3. Clear out your junk - part of the minimalist movement.

4. Remove joyless tasks and events. Or bring joy into these dull moments.

5. Explore topics that excited you as a kid.

6. Sit in silence - try to visualise and reflect.

7. Start a gratitude jar or journal.

8. Read motivating and inspiring books.

9. Get 8-9 hours of sleep a night. This helps with creation and invention in your life.

10. Feed your temple well - try eating more fresh fruits and vegetables and less sugars and processed foods.
11. Become an idea machine - write down all your ideas and inspirations.
12. Exercise and get moving more.

Daily rituals for a conscious way of life

My conscious way of life involves daily routines including meditation, energy healing, journaling and affirmations and manifestations. I also enjoy weekly contact with nature. I allow all emotions and experiences that show up in my life and I don't view them as good and bad, though rather view them as innovations of growth and learning. Instead of having control over all situations I allow myself to surrender to what is just meant to be. The best gift we can give ourselves is time spent on our own inner work. Of course it isn't easy, because inner work involves dealing with the fear, pain, resistance and all that shows up. Though usually after a breakdown always comes a breakthrough.

New vision

I have this vision to work with men, women and children individually and in sacred circles and ceremonies to create love, connection and community.

A place for conscious souls to come and feel safe, heard and loved with purpose, ritual and love. I visualise creating an eco village of healing tents and beauty where souls of all walks of life can come without judgement to heal, give birth, die, reflect and connect to mother earth. A place full of music, celebration, healers, doulas and shamans living from their heart space.

This writing is dedicated to Simon, my first love and father of my sons. Thank you for the memories, opportunities and lessons in life. I also dedicate this chapter to my parents for patiently accepting my diversity and my sister who always shines enthusiasm into my life and helped me to birth my first son into the world. I also dedicate this chapter to my precious sons, who I love unconditionally. They are my biggest teachers and mirrors in life!

Chapter 3

Alive and Kick'in
By Linda Buller

At 13 in TOWNSVILLE

My mother, my stepfather, Bill, my little brother, Kel, my sister, Georgie, and I lived in North Queensland, Australia. I was complex, curious, adventurous, concentrated, and inquisitive, but I was born with my heart stuck all over my sleeve in plain sight, a Scorpio trait, apparently, as is the opinionated big mouth. It all goes together in a little package of annoyance.

I enjoyed being at school, learning. Injustice cuts deep with me, and I couldn't understand this suffering world. Colour, space, and nature thrilled me, as well as my blue heeler dog, Clancy, and my crow, Joe. But nothing else made much sense.

This might have had something to do with being put into a room alone and not being picked up. My mum, Nancy, read a book instructing young mothers not to molly-coddle babies; you should only pick them up when you feed them. I guess that's why even now I associate food with comfort, but you know, it's all a little complex.

I was put in that room and left alone for hours.

No, I lie: the dog was there too, the black dog, Bob. I do credit Bob for encouraging humanity and humor within my soul, the part which weighs up the right and wrong. Over the years, I have teetered on the edge, the psychopath yearning to release itself. Bob nurtured my clever compassionate soul bits, enabling a momentary pause in me, so I would not murder someone on the spot, even if I thought they deserved it. Bob encouraged me to think and develop my brain and my heart. I shudder to think what I might have turned into if it weren't for brown-eyed Bob.

He loved me unconditionally, as dogs do. When I grew to toddler stage, wobbling, holding on to cot sides for support, screaming for Mum, sculpturing my shit all over the cot, he would lick off my snotty wetness, probably not the only thing he licked off, but he'd also talk until I smiled again.

Black Dog Bob: I thank him and all dogkind for my foundation of early parenting, and so should all those people who are still alive because of him.

So, in babyhood I already had a thing for animals. Bob guarded me from the moment of my birth. He growled at intruders, then talked to friends in his softer happier growl. I listened to his language and began to growl like him. I learned the different growls for different emotions and meanings. My first day at kindergarten, I wanted the swing but it was occupied by another girl. I growled loudly, engaging her eyes. That swing pretty quickly became available, much to my mother's horror. What had she brought into the world? Yes, indeed, I got the swing.

GORDON AND MUM

I had a vague warm memory of my father, Gordon.

Soon after Mum left him, the snake, Bill, came and all the nice things seemed to stop. Then all the bad things seemed to replace them. It was like Mum just gave me to him. He began my discipline, things like making me stand in corners because I was dumb. I was ignored. I was a nuisance and did not fit into the love triangle at all. The good things, like being in Mum's arms and dancing in the kitchen to a Big Band record, a snuggle in Mum's bed and having a story read, going to the shops on a Saturday morning, sauntering past the park in Bourke Road where Mum said, "John Landy trains there. He was an Australian hero, the fastest runner ever." I was so impressed.

Hand-in-hand, we'd go to the milk bar. It smelt of vanilla ice cream and cream buns. The red-faced jovial lady with a striped pink and white apron was so willing to serve, and I was allowed a marshmallow snow ball. I remember holding Mum's hand all the way there or sometimes being piggy-backed, my nostrils full of Mum's yummy hair and lipstick smells.

All those good times came to a stop.

I used to go to the kindergarten before he came, too. Every morning we were served hot milo. It was comforting and made me feel safe. A happy extravert, I climbed jungle gyms. And I heard later that my Dad, Gordon had come to see me, but they made him stand outside and look through the wire fence. Mum soon put a stop to that, though.

Once he did visit our house on Bourke Road.

He brought gifts, some Enid Blyton books. I still have those treasured items. Mum replaced Gordon—the sensitive piano player who allowed tears and expression, the handsome black-haired Irishman—with another.

My Dad was gone and replaced by a pale, blue-eyed snake who was probably good at slithering in bed, but that's all he had going for him: what he could do with his appendage was the most important thing in his mind and Mum's, I dare to say.

I'd been so proud of her though, a modern Fifties woman. She wore tweed suits to work and had a satin sky-blue dress with a halter neck for dancing, which was my favorite. In my mind, she was a princess.

She had a short cut with a long blonde piece at the front. She worked in the peace movement office, too, and so she was doing very important work, as it was the Fifties and the 2nd World War was just over. World powers were just busting for another big money war, and my mum was working for peace.

That was before we went to Townsville, the dump.

In Townsville, her work for the peace movement all stopped. She became a housewife, cleaning, cooking, making children, scrubbing floors. I wondered why. Why would you choose to be here in this dusty, hot place where no one thought about anything when all that special peace work needed to be done? But it all stopped. In this backward place, it was like the sun affected everyone and nothing much went on upstairs. World issues didn't really matter.

Anyway, everything went downhill, and I was invisible and alone. And I was angry. I knew I was useful for babysitting and other duties, though.

From the time I was six years old, there was no contact with any of my grandparents or my father. I felt different, alone. I felt self-hatred, self-doubt, and self-blame. I was moody, rebellious, depressed, confused, and sulky.

I acted out physically, fighting anyone who I thought was unfair. I would front up to have a punch on. It was a knee-jerk reaction, to just lash out.

It kept people at a distance. Just hit them hard and they stayed away. I had Dad's fast reflexes. I could duck and hit, and I always won.

When the snake would hit me and come into my bedroom uninvited while his wife was out, that's when I learned to fight for my rights, whatever I thought those were. In my opinion, it was my right to choose who was going to touch me, and I was not going to be touched by some dirty old man if I could help it.

He made sure I understood that anything that went on in his house was secret and I was never to talk to anyone outside. It was the code of silence: say nothing to anyone. Physical abuse, mental abuse, sexual abuse: say nothing. So, I was silent, but the teachers could see; they knew there was a problem.

And I did try to tell Mum.

"Mum, Bill was in my room last night. I woke up and he was touching me. He had his hand in my pants."

"What rubbish. Go to school."

"Mum, Bill was in my room again," I wanted to tell her again. But I stayed silent.

SEXUAL ABUSE

No.

Not yet.

My fingers snapped tight around the railing. Instinct strong, I wanted to survive. The back stairs would have to wait for my dead body. Another time, Grim Reaper.

I'll get out of here instead, and then life will be better.

I'm leaving. He can't touch me anymore.

I threw some clothes into my school bag.

Mum saw me. "What are you doing?"

"I'm leaving. Don't come after me or call police. If you do, you'll never see me again."

I slept downstairs under a friend's house, her parents oblivious. I was up early every morning, a wash in the weir, a chocolate bar, and off to my babysitting job.

Soon after, they saw me on the street. The slow car forced me so far off the road that I had to stop.

"Get home now," he bawled. Mum was glaring.

"Get off that bike and get home!"

"No!"

"Come on, Linda. I want to talk to you. Go home now."

"No. No, no. I won't."

"Please?"

"No. I hate it there."

"Where are you sleeping?"

"Around the place."

"Where?"

"It's not your business."

"Please, Linda. Just come. I want to talk."

Stupidly, I followed, just for Mum.

They parked. Mum came over. I waited near my bike under the stilted house. My guts shook, and I chewed the soft skin inside my lip.

"Why did you leave?"

Bill loitered, watching, slipping and slithering in the background.

Mum grilled me.

"I don't know. I don't want to be there."

She grabbed me and shook me so violently that I thought my head was about to come off, and she didn't stop.

"I already told you!" I blurted.

"Why?"

"Because he is coming into my room at night! I already told you and you ignored me.

She turned to look at him. He fell back.

"No, no, Nancy. She's…she's…she's a lying cunt."

Then mum dropped me and turned on him.

That was that.

The truth was out in the air so that everyone had to breathe it, and it made everything stink.

And it seems it was ALL my fault.

And now I was really loathed. I'd upset the bloody apple cart and there was rotten apples all over the place.

Of course, I was forced to stay there. I was expected to still live there, to babysit, to help around like nothing had ever happened.

"I'm not going to break up my family because of this," Mum said. So…

Because I'd always been so desperate for her love, I would do anything to have a pat on the head or a nod of approval, but I realized this was not ever going to happen. I asked her to let me leave. I could go to boarding school or to Melbourne and be with Nanna. I wanted to be able to study and to be somebody.

"No, you can't, Linda," she said. Okay, I'll wait, I thought. First opportunity, I'm gone.

She told me I had to stay and go to school and forget about Bill. But he lived in the same house. How could I forget about him?

He kept trying to come into my room, and I kept trying to protect myself. He was violent and jealous. I had to learn to fight and strategize. One night, I was asleep and he dragged me off my bunk. He had both of my legs dangling over the side of the bed so he could perform cunnilingus, and he had his fingers up me just to check. He said, "Oh, you're too small." My sister was asleep on the bottom bunk, or I would have screamed. I needed to protect her, too.

After a few more incidents, I was on to him, and I would listen for when Mum left the house and get downstairs immediately. Then I would go into the front yard with a brick and I would swear at him and tell him I would scream if he tried to touch me, and then everyone would know.

One day we had a full-on punch up. He got too close to the stairs, and I landed a good kick and down he went. Victory!

After that, he'd walk around me at a distance, scowling, because I was so angry and full of rage and revenge and hatred and self-loathing and heartache and resentment. Why was I having to be in this horrible house? What did I ever do to deserve being here, and then to be blamed for this bastard's abuse?

CLANCY DIED

One day after I came home from school when I didn't think my life could be any worse, Don, the weird man from the house over the road, said, "Is that your mongrel dog down there dead as a door nail on the foot path?" And he had a good old laugh. "Good riddance to the mongrel."

I ran breathlessly.

Clancy lay on the footpath, a bloody mess. Yes, he was dead. I fell down next to him.

I lifted his lips, kissed his head, and held him. His tongue was blue and cold, and his supple body was stiff. His spirit was gone. His pink happy tongue stopped, and his loving eyes glazed and he was gone.

He had died alone. My best friend was gone.

Abandoned and in real pain, how would I move through this grief? I did not know. Who knows at that age?

So I labeled it and filed it for later. And I got on with surviving life. But I was mad.

Fucking death.

Fuck death.

SEARCHING

I feel more like a dog than a human, and I'd rather be a dog. Dogs are more fair and happy. They love life. They don't kill for no reason or try to screw their babies. And they don't have resentments. Most importantly, they have the rare ability to love unconditionally. If I ever meet humans with that quality, I always wonder if they were a dog in their last life.

So, I want to be like a dog.

Self-hate soaked me up. I'm a misfit, a fucking nuisance, and dumb as.

I should not have been born. I should be dead.

But I'm not dead. I'm here, and unless I kill myself I have to learn to toughen up. And that's what I had to do. But there was so much to carry, a very large trailer load of baggage, of hurt, of pain and anger, and all the self-flagellating shit that I could not put anywhere. I couldn't hide it. I just had to live with it.

I felt Mum just didn't want to give me the time of day. I have learned we all have our limits. Maybe I was just too much to cope with.

Painting was good for me. I started to paint a lot. Poetry class took me to another realm: Shakespeare and Donne among others, listening for answers. And then I heard it.

"Death, be not proud…"

Our lecturer dissected the verse. It seemed that Donne thought that death could be beaten.

I pondered and analyzed and concluded that he was just deluding himself and that death and nothingness would be the victor. And that became a fundamental fact.

I kept painting and writing. It kept me from trying to figure everything out. I was filled with confusion, self-hatred, and disillusionment, but I still painted and wrote hope.

I could see good in the world: the love my grandfather had for my grandmother, people fighting for human rights. I remembered the peace office in Melbourne where there were good people. Then I'd swing back to feeling there is nothing and no point.

Did I ask to be born?

NO.

Well maybe I did.

THE PARTY

I had a gin and lemonade at a party. It tasted nice. In fact, it was great! I didn't realize it was gin. I thought it was just a nice drink, and I kept drinking.

I was quickly paralytic and found myself being held by other teens over a sink being made to swallow salt water to induce vomiting.

Graham, my boyfriend, took advantage of the situation. My first bit of sex was in a bed in a strange house where others came in at the party and backed out of the room quickly when they realized what the gyrating was beneath the covers. I don't really remember much of it.

Arriving home, I snuck into the house. There were no lights on, and as I tiptoed into my dark room the light suddenly glared into my eyes and Mum's face was an inch from mine, too too close.

She snarled, "You've been drinking."

Why was she sitting in the dark in my room? Her eyes sliced glaringly into me. My legs began to shake. I cowered. My head screamed, "Save yourself! Get away!"

I turned to climb up to my bed hoping she wouldn't grab me from behind. I climbed fast up and onto my bunk, safe. I curled up small in my sleeping bag. And waited for sleep.

A few days later, Graham came around. I walked pushing my bike with him on the street. I wanted to finish it with him. Then Bill saw us. He stopped his car and said, "Get over here, bitch."

"No."

He came straight at me, grabbing at me. Graham stood there helpless. I had to defend myself. Was he going to stand up to Bill?

I waited, and waited, till the last minute, and then I grabbed the bike pump and dropped my bike.

I stood strong. I knew I could get the first one in, but the next?

As he came close, I swung and slammed him hard. Blood spurted from his face. His hand went to his head. Then he went to the boot and took out the crank handle, a piece of iron used for cranking a dead engine. "Let's see if this doesn't change your mind," he snarled. He flourished his weapon.

Graham just stood there gaping.

"Right," I thought. "Here we go." And I started to freak.

Just then, a couple of rockers in leather coats came out of a house.

"Hey," one of them called out. "Put that thing down or we'll wrap it around your head."

"She's my daughter. I'll do what I like."

"We don't care who she is. Get going or we'll do ya."

Great. A couple of strangers stood up for me.

Strangers.

Graham?

Life was too hard. That lump in my throat would not dislodge itself.

I'M PREGNANT

At 16, Graham became an expectant father. "Graham, you have to help," I said. "I need to have an abortion."

"Sorry."

Can't do..Don't know…

Useless.

Doctor said, "You made your bed, girly. Now you can lie in it." I was nauseous and vomiting. I started working at the army barracks climbing up ladders and cleaning windows. The metho made me retch. I made some wages. I hoped I could make enough in time, images of that Dr and his sadistic smirk, when I asked for an abortion, "we don't do that here",

a brick wall...

One day, Bill started again: "You slut. You harlot. You wouldn't get a place in a brothel. You bludger."

I felt so ill. I screamed at mum, "Why don't you ever defend me? I am so sick of this! You just let this happen to your own daughter?"

I really screamed. I think the house rocked.

She turned and stared at me. "What's wrong with you? You always protect yourself."

Then she said it.

"Are you pregnant?"

"Yes, I am!" I yelled.

She took me aside and asked what I wanted to do.

"Really? You are asking me? You really want to hear me?" I was stunned. She actually listened.

"I can't look after myself, can I? How am I to take care of a baby? I need to have an abortion."

"Okay," she said. And she called her brother, Jock, in Melbourne.

"Linda's coming down for an abortion."

I met with Graham. I wanted to finish it. He cried and fell on the grass at the park and said he could not live, etc. I relented so that he would feel better, but I knew it was over.

I got on a train, the *Sunlander*. I hadn't wanted to have sex, and I didn't want to be travelling miles away to have an abortion; this was not my idea of a good beginning to life. I wanted to be in university and studying to become a vet or a doctor, even though I thought I was too dumb to pass those kinds of exams. Yes, I wanted out of Townsville, but not like this. I had not been interested in sex, but I had allowed my boyfriend to go full bore as I'd gotten so depressed and he was the only person

I thought that would give me some stability. Plus, he never shut up about wanting a bit and how I was his life and how much he loved me and how he could never be with anyone else, etc., etc.

All words, just words…

I'd like to just rewind back to the party that night.

I slept on the floor of the train for four days and nights and two thousand miles. Uncle Jock was waiting on the platform.

I stared at the city lights. Oh, so nice to be home! It felt like I'd arrived. My uncle just wrapped his arms around me. We hopped in the car. I let the mesmerizing city lights of Melbourne warm my soul, and I was free.

A week after the abortion, I went to dinner at Dorothy Gibson's, one of Mum's friends from the peace movement. With her encouragement and help searching the phone book, she pointed to a name. "That's him! That's Gordon, your dad! There you are, Linda. That's Gordon's number. Call him."

"No, it's okay."

She wouldn't have it. "Call him. I'm here. It will be okay. Call him."

I hesitantly picked up the phone.

It rang one, two, three times. Then…

"Hello." I heard a nice male voice. Was this my dad?

"Hello?"

"Yes? Who's this? And how may I help you?"

"I'm your daughter. I'm Linda." He was silent.

It was amazing that we were still connected. And what's more, I look exactly like him. As some say, "She's spit out of his mouth, that one." And, "The apple didn't fall far from the tree, that one. She's the spittin' image of her Dad, she is."

Irish, musical and funny, warm, loving: all spruced up, he came to my grandmother's gate. I'll never forget that day. I waited near the bay window, then on the porch, then at the window again. I hopped around waiting to see him. Then he was there. How could I ever forget? He stood at the wire gate—tie, white shirt, black pants, his hair combed and all in place, warm hazel eyes appraising me, black cow lick, dimples when he smiled, a picture of handsomeness—and in his arms was a huge box with a pink silk ribbon. He came up the stair and stopped in front of me.

"Are you my beautiful daughter?" he asked gently.

I nodded.

And he put his arms around me. This was the best day I ever had until then and now.

He placed the huge box of pink carnations in my arms. He was my prince, and I was in his arms: the girl who wasn't worth protecting, the girl who was allowed to be biffed and wacked around in her mother's house, the girl who was rubbish and who was to be used for the step-man's snake's pleasure, bullied laughed at, accused of making a spectacle of herself, the girl who was an inconvenience to everyone, a mistake, unlovable.

On that day, Gordon asked if he could play my grandparents' piano. He came in and played,

"Lindy, did you hear that mocking bird sing last night"

I was named after that song, and I'm forever grateful I met my darling father. Even though I only got to see him for a short time, he helped me to know I was worth being loved. And even now I still carry that precious memory. It helps me to heal my heart.

Gordon's embrace and tenderness was not expected. His generosity, love for me, and his innate knowing and acceptance of this manifestation of ugliness was all unforeseen, but there I was wrapped in his arms, my head nestled in his strong gentle fatherliness, and there I cried. Trust entered and stayed within this place where my father's heart was. There, I found joy and laughter. Only eight years on, he died unexpectedly at the age of 50. My best friend and only ally…unbridled devastation abandonment…

In the meantime, I had married a man with a big drinking problem, and we had a little boy I needed to protect and care for. I had no job and no house, and my sister and brother refused to recognize me, even though Dad had not forgotten me.

I was included in his will, but my darling Dad had not signed it. And even though my name was on the grave stone as being one of his kids, something I am so proud of, and his intention was known, I was again abandoned in all ways. Not a thing did cross from them to me. Dad had worked hard and had accrued property, etc. Even the shop where I'd lived with Mum and Dad as a baby was still there, and to this day is in my brother's and sister's possession. They have an income from it. But not even the chair could I have, the chair that my mother had bought him and he had reupholstered to keep her memory alive. Not the piano, not a photo, not a letter was I entitled to or given. The photos of Dad and I were disposed of.

I took myself back to school. I went to Bendigo Institute of Technology to earn a fine arts diploma, to be that artist and make something of myself. I was also smoking a lot of dope, drinking, and partying. It was the thing to do, especially if you had a lot of other friends doing the same. I left my husband of four years.

One day, after 20 years had passed me by, I realized my son had left home. My next husband left me, too. Going to pubs every night was not his idea of life, apparently.

I had set up and was still running a pretty successful massage service, which I called Above Board Massage. I looked after many hotels in Melbourne and had many VIP clients. I even massaged Ben Kingsley, Nina Simone, Sarah Bernhard, Lou Reed, and many more well-known people.

That business could have provided me the best life if I had stayed with it. I had so much work, and it was the only hotel massage service in town. I employed over 20 masseurs. It worked, but the marriage breakup crippled me. I could not stop crying; I would try to massage someone, and all my tears would be dribbling onto their skin. I could not stop. So, I went to a therapist. He said, "Well, thank your lucky stars he's gone. You were being mentally abused and you don't know what love is because you'd never had it in your home of origin."

All of those stars I had massaged, all of those invites to all their shows: they must have seen something in me, I thought.

I felt like I was living in a morgue, so silent was my house, and so empty.

One day I was looking through all my photos and letters, and I was appalled. I had achieved nothing. Why was I here? I'd done nothing but a few paintings, and they meant nothing. I had gone to university and completed a diploma of Traditional Chinese Medicine, but that did not make me feel better. In 1986, I had painted a huge mural on a Preston Market Place wall for the International Year of Peace and had been paid by the Preston Council, but that didn't mean anything. I was alone and I felt I had to do something or I would have to put a stop to it.

One last chance, I thought, and I launched myself with the last bit of hope I had left.

On the Dole

I went to the dole office and got the dole payment. It wasn't much. I'd lost my business, my marriage, my son, and everything else. My sanity seemed in question. The booze and dope was all I really had left. That and the dole.

After my husband deserted me, I left, too. I decided to not live in that silent house with all its shattered dreams, the walls constantly yawning all my deepest regrets.

I had to fix everything. I had about three grand, and so I decided to buy a caravan and go to Broome, many kilometers away. I drew "Broome or Bust" on the back window of the van.

A memory kept nagging, a vivid dream I'd had eight years previously. A spirit had come to my bedside and said, "My name is Kusamba, and if you want to solve all your problems, go to BROOME." I decided now to follow that advice. What else could I do? I had to buy a car to pull the van. I went to the auctions in Victoria Street, and there was an old automatic Kingwood station wagon. I knew it had to be a manual, not an automatic, but I could not resist the blue. It was a lovely blue. Cheap, too. A big mistake, because the van was too heavy for it, but it WAS a beautiful blue.

I Bought supplies

Off I went. The car over heated within 60 km, smoke billowing out of the engine. The gear box was too hot. I was stuck on the highway.

I stopped for the night, my dogs and cats with me. What a mess! But I kept on the next day, stopping a lot, and arrived in Ballarat. And that's where I had to stay for the winter. The car could not take me any farther.

I was stuck in this deserted caravan park with the bad tempered, frumpy female who ran it and her miserable cross-eyed I-don't-trust-you stare. The freezing ground in the mornings were of white ice crackling underfoot on the path to the wash rooms, just me and my dogs and an old drunk across the way, bottle in brown paper bag. I would rarely see him otherwise, only as he scurried to the toilet.

But I had a computer and I was a writer and an artist. I was making something of myself with my flagons of wine and my joints and my delusions.

I stood outside one morning, the gum trees swaying above, the sun out and warming the soul, a soft eucalyptus breeze. I was deep in thought, wondering how I could get out of there. I had nothing left, just a piece of bread and a tomato in a sandwich. I was just bringing it up to my mouth when, low and behold, it disappeared.

A clever magpie had spied that tomato, a tasty tidbit, he thought, and swooping fast, he precisely plucked the tomato out of my bread. I was left bewildered. A dry piece of bread and a message from God in the form of a bird…

What the fuck are you doing, Linda?

There was something really wrong with this picture.

I went to the dole office and got my next pay, then turned around and headed back to the farm. It was all downhill from Ballarat, and uphill to Mum's farm. God must have been there, because the car did not overheat going up the mountain, and it should have.

I arrived, but I was not acceptable.

Mum's boyfriend, Bruno, said, "You're an alcoholic."

I said, "So are you."

My mother said, "We don't need you here."

I said, "I don't want to be here, either."

Soon afterwards my house sold. I had 13 thousand dollars. At the farm, in the van, I had no electricity, no water, and nowhere else to go. My drinking had escalated and depression had almost consumed me.

Nothing had changed. I was still fucking useless, a waste of space, an inconvenience. I was not welcome in the house, and I realized it was stupid to wait for anything to change. I had to get out. I knew I was seen as the rubbish bin where everyone could throw all of their unwanted shit and blame.

I got away! I DID get away! It's called a geographical, where everything will be better after I get out of here.

And so I bought a one-way ticket and took my miserable shitty self to Bali.

I only had 12 thousand dollars now to do me for the rest of my life. I found a run-down cheap room. The roof leaked and a rat lived in the cupboard. I put the cat in there. Go on cat: get the rat! It sat with disdain and licked itself, then lazily left the rat to do its business.

That rat nibbled my hair at night and slept on my pillow, I'm sure. I bought a motor bike. Transportation had drained my bank balance, and I had to have enough funds to buy wine. It was expensive.

I went to a friend's party on Christmas Day. I went and I drank, but I couldn't get drunk. I went to another party on Boxing Day, and I drank a lot, but I couldn't get drunk. When I got back to my room, the floor was flooded. The broken glass bottle I had noticed was probably still upstairs on the porch. I could slash my neck. I knew how to do that. I turned to go up there, but it was too far and it was raining and dark and I might kill myself going up the stairs, before I could kill myself.

And so I sloshed to the bed and fell in with the rat.

At the pub, I cried a lot. One or two glasses, and I would start. Every time I drank a wine, it all got worse. I would talk about my childhood stolen by the snake. I was sick of myself being always in the pity pot.

Grey-haired Jack, one of the locals, piped up and said, "Well, Linda, if you're tired of crying and drinking, if you're sick of this grief, go and get help."

"Where, Jack? Where can I go?"

"There's a meeting up the road in Ubud. Go there."

He said the right thing at the right time. I heard him. So, I did go.

I remember that in 1986 I had come to Bali for a holiday. One very hot day, I saw this poor thing staggering, and shaking its head. It stopped me in my tracks. This poor animal's head had been sliced off. Her brain was exposed to the sun, and she was still staggering.

"Oh, no!" I exclaimed frantically to the Balinese man close by. "Who can help this dog? We have to help her! Her brain is exposed, and she is suffering. She needs to be put to sleep."

"No one can help," he said and laughed. "She must have forgot to put her helmet on."

He said, "Doctor for dog! No have doctor for Dog, you crazy lady!"

He exclaimed, and loud laughter exploded from him again. I was dumbfounded, but a plan began to build itself.

They were on their own, our best friends. If they were sick, starving, injured, too bad. It was the survival of the fittest. Amidst all my rage and self-abuse and self-disgust there erupted this burning empathy for the maltreated, the vulnerable, the neglected. And, in that moment, my destiny became clear.

RECOVERY

That poor animal's suffering had never left my mind, and now I could do what I wanted. I wanted to make a safe place for the abandoned dogs in Bali. Twelve years in Australia had dragged me to my knees. To make it possible for me to return to DO something, I had to crawl.

I went to my first meeting on 27 December 1998, when Jack had suggested it. After that meeting, I heard that I would never have to drink again. I received many gifts, a new family, self-respect, a loving higher power, and a new positive way to live this life.

And during my first year of sobriety, I began to rescue them, the sad thrown-away puppies. I think I was rescuing myself by loving them.

I wanted to paint, but every time I saw a suffering animal, I suffered, too. I would scoop them up into a bag and take them home and give TLC and meds.

For 17 years, there were no vaccinated dogs in Bali. If they suffered distemper, they just died horribly. I bought vaccines and began to vaccinate. There were so many viruses. The place was rife with all sorts of nasty diseases.

Pretty quickly, I had 20 dogs.

The first dog was Wang. Emaciated and fully grown, I found her hanging out in front of Casa Luna, a well-off restaurant where no one, not even the owners, looked at her sideways. Hairless, her skin was like leather, baked black and hard and stretched over her protruding hip bones. She was starving, and no one—no tourist, no expatriate—no one even looked at her.

Well, I got her home, and she lasted a couple of weeks. Warm beds, meds, and lots of food and love could not save her. She was way too broken. She died only two weeks later.

Then I found Ming. Ming was a white Bali puppy bravely following her mother down the main street. It looked like she had been kicked in the head. She was injured and so small.

She grew into a sweetheart and claimed herself a chair. She'd lie back and watch everything from a distance. She was a sweet observer. I had her for 10 years.

I was told by some not to set up any place for dogs. It would cost too much. There was too much against it: disease, no real vets, etc.

I listened. But, no. I decided I would just do what I wanted.

I found a place, a run-down gallery, and some Balinese boys to help, and we built cement cubicles for the pups. I kept them in isolation for a month. They would have two complete vaccinations. I found a vet who had learned sterilization, as well. It was not perfect, but it was the best we could do at the time. Then I would look for homes and release them to travel their own karmic roads.

I never stopped painting and writing stuff through all the years.

I lost many friends. As many as 40 have died of overdoses, cancer, heartbreak, and suicide. But I'm still here. I ask myself how and why. My grandfather was a stretcher bearer in the First World War. He wondered, too, after four years of dodging bullets and seeing a lot of friends being blown to bits, why he had survived without one bit of shrapnel. Why was he still allowed to come home and have a wife, to marry and have kids and live out his older years when so many had lost their lives? I just think it all means that we get given so much shit that we need to learn from, and when it's unbearable, it stops. Or maybe it gets worse. God, I don't know, but I wonder why I'm so lucky or unlucky and still here.

In early sobriety, I still cried a lot from frustration, rage, and grief. I was easily overwhelmed. But I knew that, as long as I was alive, I had a chance to get myself right. I had begun to take care of my own heart, to try and be gentle with others, and to give what I had to others who wanted help.

We humans can get well and do good things and be strong and stand up for the good stuff.

I have to pinch myself sometimes, because basically I'm happy. I have a wonderful life today, and I'm feeling fulfilled. I'm useful and I am so much more healed. I even like myself, and I feel like I have achieved something good for my best friends, both the four-legged and the two-legged ones. I'm not the rubbish, as I once thought. I'm a poet, an artist, a doctor of Chinese Medicine, a humanitarian, an animal lover, a comedian, a tram driver, a mother, a wife, a good friend, a loving sister and daughter, a lover of this beautiful world, a fighter for good against evil, a feminist… I talk to Gordon almost every day. I hope he can hear me. I call my mother regularly and stay in touch with friends and family.

I also have a family of inner soul explorers, humans with courage and love and intuition and self-discipline and integrity. I'm loved, and I can love and trust. And I have learned to allow my heart to forgive.

Life's a slog. We have many mountains to climb. I gave up full-time painting, my healing clinic, travelling, etc., in order to fight for my four-legged friends. And I would do it all again just to see them smile and to see those tails wag.

Today I paint and exhibit. I have a healing clinic in Bali, and I am learning to speak publicly about the marvelous Bali Heritage Dogs who are struggling to survive so that the world will know just how special they are.

I want we humans to remember that the bad times will pass.

Remember: don't give up on yourself, because from the real shit grows the best and strongest flowers. Life is never easy, but we can ask for help in the right places, and we can do good no matter how hurt and bashed up we have been.

We recover. Humans are like that: resilient. And we have that deep positive ingredient. It's called hope.

Now, many years later, we have a place for the suffering animals here. It's called BARC: Bali (dog) Adoption Rehabilitation Center.

We also have a sanctuary surrounded by green rice fields and cool breezes in the Bali mountains for our rescues, the ones no one wants. They get live out their lives in peace. It's called Warriors Legacy after my dear late friend, Anna, and her husband.

BARC attests to a little girl who was hurt and lost and was loved by dogs and who refused to do what others told her to do.

BARC is a testament to good humans standing up against cruelty and injustice, a testament to the love of humans and animals together and how love can conquer all that's negative and replace it with joy and goodness.

When humans realize and act on the fact that we are caretakers of this earth, we are obliged to rule with compassion, humanity, and courage. Then it will be a better world for all concerned.

And my life's healing owes huge gratitude to a 12-step program where I found my spiritual family and where I learned that we all have a higher power which loves each and every one of us.

St. Frances's Prayer

Lord, make me an instrument of your peace:
where there is hatred, let me sow love;
where there is injury, pardon;
where there is doubt, faith;
where there is despair, hope;
where there is darkness, light;
where there is sadness, joy.
O divine Master, grant that I may not so much seek
to be consoled as to console,
to be understood as to understand,
to be loved as to love.
For it is in giving that we receive,
it is in pardoning that we are pardoned,
and it is in dying that we are born to eternal life.
Amen.

Chapter 4

Lessens Embedded in Life by Scott Cohen

I was raised in a middle-class neighborhood, in the suburbs of Los Angeles, by a father and a mother who were college educated and living the American dream. My father was an electronic engineer, a product of the WWII GI Bill, and one of the pioneers in the booming aerospace and electronics industries. My mother, a runway model and newly indoctrinated Avon Lady, was a stay-at-home mom raising four children on a shoestring budget. I was number three out of four, never feeling a lack of love from my mother. As children, we either rode our bikes or walked to school during the elementary years, but during middle school years, we were driven to school and back home by either my mom or a friend's mom. High school years were influential to the extent of advanced History and English courses. Sports were important to me, including baseball, basketball, and wrestling teams.

What was missing in my life? Well, looking back I vividly remember the love I got from my father was in the form of historical facts and not the adulation that you feel from a father who hugs and kisses you and says, "I love you." During these years of my life, I never questioned his behavior as a lack of love but believed it was just how fathers show love with their children. It was an unsaid thing and I just knew my dad loved me!

This lack of childhood adulation would later be apparent in my life. But as a prepubescent child playing with friends, I recall having my mom yell into the bowels of the neighborhood, "Scott! It's Time for Dinner!" This was the call I either loathed, as I was having so much fun and wishing the day would never end, or made me extremely excited, as the hunger pangs fluttered throughout my belly and I was going to wolf that food down and then watch my favorite black and white or color television shows.

Television played an important part in shaping my outlook on society and my place in it. I loved to watch time travel fantasy shows, shows about space travel, historical events, cartoons to an extent, the primetime family shows that contained issues addressing race relations, religion, and integration, most public broadcasting, and a lot of news.

An important part of my life centered around the dinner table, where discussions of my day in school were open to comments from my brother and sister. My oldest sister was typically incarcerated or away at some camp for "bad children," and so an attempt by my parents to have dinner to be peaceful was a futile attempt at best forty percent of the time. The remainder of the time, we discussed the day-to-day goings-on of a typical American family, such as interactions with friends and whether or not there was anyone special we might like from school.

Common among our discussions was me standing up for a kid at school that was either African American, Latino, or just one of the kids who was picked on because he or she seemed weak. This was who I was, and I was not afraid to take a stand for those who could not stand for themselves. *This would be my core value in life, and today it is who I am.*

My parents' liberal views on race, religion, and politics shaped my opinions and worldview and would carry on into my later years in life, and they would help to influence me in the choices of who I would and still do associate with in life. My parents mainly associated with their friends from the years they lived in Hollywood during the 1950s. These were Hollywood actors, musicians, poets, and writers. Some famous Hollywood stars would be at our home and would go out with my parents, but us kids never knew any better, nor did we really care to know. As a family, we had a diversity of friends, a real reflection of my parents practicing what they preached, surely a reflection of what we, their children, would adopt in our own lives. Friendships with local families, ranging from Italians and Jewish families, Filipinos and African American families, determined where we went on weekend getaways and special dinners and—most importantly—picnics. We were living the American Dream, the true American experience!

Cousins were a scarcity, as they lived far away in the southern part of California or back east in the New York State area. We only visited cousins back east twice in my lifetime, but we saw the California cousins about four times a year. One time while we were in New York, one of my cousins challenged me to dive into a two-foot deep plastic pool. I accepted the challenge and broke my nose. This event was one in a line of challenges that *would shape who I would become in life*: this adolescent decision to dive into two feet of water face first!

Now, as much as family was important to us, the five of us were a tight-knit unit that protected each other as much as our abilities allowed.

Junior High School

The junior high school years were more formative than the prior seven grades, from girls on my mind 24/7 to sports, music, education, and pot smoking. The girls were a wonder and a challenge to me, as I tried to figure out if they were just being fickle, or if they liked me and were playing coy. This quagmire I eventually figured out, thus enabling me to *communicate with girls on a deeper level*, and benefiting me in all sorts of areas in my youth. Still, today, I possess that ability. The joy of kissing a girl was probably the most pleasurable thing to me while still maintaining my youthful innocence.

This time in my life was a tipping point for my creativity, as *I developed a steadfast determination to be right* and was driven to be top in all sports in which I competed. Sports were so important to me, as I played baseball and basketball. Football was a passion of mine, as well, but my father insisted that football players were too likely to sustain concussions, ultimately causing brain damage. (Boy! Did he have insight!) He would point to older professionals that became non-ambulatory or used a cane once they retired, showing me my future if I just looked at the *short-term satisfaction* of playing a game and *ignored the unintended consequences* of my actions.

This lesson would serve me well later in life, even though I was missing out on the enjoyment of the game of football. Baseball and basketball were a different story. The team effort was the important part of the game to me, even though I received accolades as an all-star athlete in both sports. Going to state championships made me so proud as a kid in California. This combination of highly recognized individual achievements and team successes, would soon define my childhood. What do I mean exactly? Because I played sports all the time? Yes, I played sports all the time, and that defined me as a *competitive, driven, and determined boy.*

As much as I loved sports, music was and is still my most cherished passion. I would not only spend my weekly allowance on baseball cards and hot dogs but also by going down the block to the music store to purchase a 45" single record with a flip side. This was the early-to-mid-seventies, and popular music, along with soul and rock, had become a sex-and-drug innuendo style of music, reflecting my life to a tee. I was listening to and growing my record collection immensely, listening to later-year Beatles, James Brown, Wilson Picket, Led Zeppelin, Cream, and lots of popular radio stars. This was to be the ending of my childhood innocence in musical taste and the transition into a more sophisticated jazz-oriented and thought-provoking part of my life.

My teachers in junior high were influential to me, as they pressed me to see if I was stretching my capabilities. I was maybe 60% of the time. My grades were reflective of the effort I put into my schoolwork, achieving B's mainly, not my fullest potential. There would be a fundamental shift in this learning process, but that would occur in high school and would prove to be monumental.

Now smoking pot was a recreation that my friends and I enjoyed immensely. I loved the thrill of not getting caught with an illicit drug, but I could not get into being high! This was apparently a mixture of thrills, and the social pressure of leading the groups I associated with. These characteristics have been with me my entire life, serving me well in many ways, but being a self-imposed leader would be to my detriment, as *expectations of myself were, and still are, set so high* that I frequently experience self-doubt and a lack of self-acknowledgement. Looking back on this phase of my life, I see how pot smoking hindered my learning process and prevented me from reaching my full potential in school. Fortunately, sports were not affected, as the two activities never occurred simultaneously.

High School

High school years were a whole different ball of wax. These times were about sex, drugs, and rock and roll. I partied before school at times, on weekends, and after baseball and basketball games. Drugs did not interfere with my performance of sports, nor did they cause me to underperform in my studies. What they did was to open my eyes to the self-deprecation of drug use in my early twenties.

I played baseball and basketball and was on the wrestling team. I was accepted by most in high school but was not considered a jock, as I had started what was to become a co-major in college and was a dancer and live performer. Although music was still my most prized passion, playing an instrument was something I was not committed to learning. However, dancing to music fulfilled my need to participate in music and opened a whole new world for me: the entertainment industry. I started off by infrequently taking ballet and jazz dance classes and learning swing dancing from my parents as a side note. Disco had taken hold of society worldwide, thus catapulting me into teaching disco at adult parties and getting paid. This was my indoctrination into capitalism. I even went to underage discos, so that I could keep up with the latest dance steps. And, of course, meet girls! So, getting girls was never a problem; staying in a committed relationship, I was not too keen on.

Sports in high school took me to a whole new level by teaching me new skills while strengthening me for my dance career, which was soon to follow. Although I was a six-foot-tall white kid, I could barely push the basketball into the rim, technically not considered a slam dunk, but I was able to jump so high that my dance skills furthered immensely. At this point, I knew that dance was my thing. I ignored the innuendos thrown at me from the jocks while thriving in my relationships with the girls, who knew what a straight male dancer could offer a rapidly maturing young lady. I even dated college girls that looked at me curiously, as they knew I was different from the other boys. In fact, many of my friends went to discos with me, to learn what I'd learned and to find new girlfriends as well. The high school experience would serve me well into my college years by taking these exciting and adventurous thirty-six months of childhood-ending times and opening my eyes to all the possibilities my life had to offer.

From the ages of fifteen to eighteen I always had a paying job. I was a janitor, a cook, a shoe salesman, a bus boy, and a waiter. All jobs were part-time and allowed me to continue my studies, date girls, take dance classes, play sports, and go out to discos and live it up. These early job years helped to establish my work ethic and drive to better myself in life and my future career. Being fired from only one job established in me *consistency and dependability*, and that is structurally who I am as a person. These jobs were so memorable that, even today, I can still recall weeks of memories at a time. Selling shoes to celebrities in Century City and Beverly Hills were some of the best times in my life, as they prepared me for larger ticket items, such as working with home mortgages, which I still do today as part of my reinvented self. Some of my more memorable clients were African royalty that spent at least $3,000 at a time on ladies' shoes when they were an average of $100 a pair. You see, I still had insight with women, and that served me well. Seems like I had an eye for fashion and capitalism as well.

College

Once I was out of high school and into college, I was soon earning a living working and dancing full-time. I participated in dance performances, which were mainly college and Los Angeles theatre stage. Some were even paying jobs as a dancer and choreographer. School was squeezed in with a full load, and my grades were easily maintained because my cognitive abilities had been enhanced through athletic discipline and the fact that I was now living a fully drug-free life. All of this multitasking took up so much of my time that I only had time for sex with women whom I met thru my dance companies and classes. This was one of the most unfulfilling periods with women in my life. While I was a double major in college (Dance and History), my survival instincts started kicking in, and, by the time I was twenty-five, my dance career was over, which left me as a five-year college non-graduate shoe salesman with no career path. I did eventually have a steady girlfriend for an eight-year period, and she was an influential part of my life, an important part of me becoming a real man. Soon my luck would turn for the better.

Early Career

I ultimately got a job with Nordstrom, who was expanding their US presence from the Washington area down into Southern California. There, I started off selling ladies' shoes, but that was not enough. I figured out that, since two other high-end department stores in Beverly Hills had a wardrobe division which catered to the television and movie studios, I could create that division within the Nordstrom family. That I did, while assembling a team of three other employees to work alongside of me. We became the Nordstrom Wardrobe Division. With the blessing of the CEO of Nordstrom, I went out and personally met with studio executives of NBC, CBS, ABC, Paramount, and other small movie lots in the Hollywood area, generating unlimited credit lines for these ventures and was granted full access to many shows and their stars. I not only would sell two to five duplicate outfits for each actor, as outfits would tear or get destroyed, but I also developed personal relationships with the wardrobe stylists and eventually the actors themselves.

My clientele base was becoming well established, and my income was exponentially increasing. Here is where my *entrepreneurial bug* started, all while working within a corporate environment! I soon realized that an established brand name such as Nordstrom had to be *earned and not expected*. This work ethic and business philosophy has been with me ever since those Nordstrom years. In fact, I realized that a good reputation in business could easily be negated by just one bad customer experience. In other words, *you're only as good as your last deal!* This mantra is part of all my business modelling and business plans that I create today. It has also been the negative driving force that I create when I don't trust that someone will get the job done, and so I do it myself. In my career, this has held me back from making an imprint on America on a larger scale. I have been a lone wolf, and that is great for a twenty- or-fewer-employee mom and pop shop, but not for a national corporation.

In the late eighties, I decided that I would change directions and develop a career in some type of outside sales, as I seemed to be successful at attracting clients in a one-on-one sales environment. So, I got a job selling BMW's, which provided me a completely different experience in sales. This job taught me how to read people more effectively. I learned more about decision-making on the spot when dealing with high-ticket items. In fact, I figured that whoever bought expensive cars might offer me a different type of sales job that could pay me over six figures if I were persistent enough and would just simply ask for a job!

Well, that's exactly what happened, and after a four-month stint at selling BMW's, I was now a loan officer for a California-based mortgage lender. This was the beginning of what was to be my life in financial services. I started out by learning about government loans—Fannie Mae and Freddie Mac—and eventually worked with jumbo loans valuing into the millions. My skills had served me well, and now I knew what I really wanted to do as an adult and eventually as a family man.

I worked as an outside loan officer, which meant going out into the field and calling on realtors for business, bringing in the loans, and preparing a loan package for my loan processor. I had to know how to put a loan together that was designated for a specific lender when brokering and for an investor when we closed the loan ourselves. I eventually processed my loans by myself, a true reflection of who I was as a lone wolf, not trusting others when it came to my reputation. This served me well at the time, as I created self-reliant charts of various lenders/investors guidelines so that I could easily place a loan with various risk factors with multiple channels, ultimately maximizing my time and obtaining the appropriate and best pricing for my client.

Family

At this point in my life, I met my now-wife, Merced! I proposed marriage after dating just four months, and we've never stopped growing. Our honeymoon period lasted over five years, and we cherish those early years, as our 26th year of marriage and partnership has been a wonderful journey for the ages. We went on vacation after vacation, traveling through various parts of the US, and visited other countries as well. We partied (no drugs) until all hours of the night, all while making lots of money.

After just one year of marriage, we decided to take our relationship to a new level by having kids. We had our first child, a daughter, and we named her Paige. We knew from day one that she was going to be a creative, empathetic, and powerful woman, and boy were we right! Our second child was a boy, and we named him Tanner. He was, and is, a powerful, vulnerable, and compassionate man. The years while they were small children were filled with so much joy and gave us a sense of completeness. We were bathing in the wonderment of our children's life experiences, comparing them to our own very different upbringings, while instilling in them the values that our parents had taught us. We learned a lot from our children, especially what it meant to prioritize their lives ahead of our own. We soon had new friends, usually parents of our kids' friends from school and extracurricular activities, such as baseball, basketball, and camp.

Turbulent Years

Soon my career had developed to a point where I learned to underwrite loans, which broadened my knowledge base and thirst for more information, so that I could be well-rounded and upgrade my career. Eventually, while raising our children, Merced and I decided that it was okay for me to go out on my own and start my own mortgage company. I did, and it thrived for many years, offering residential, commercial, and multi-family loans to individuals and small businesses.

At this point, I did not want to look back, but soon I was forced to go to work for a larger California-based direct mortgage lender. This job was as a wholesale lender, serving the mortgage broker community. I grew the sales force to national prominence with alternative products. This was the break I needed to stop playing lone wolf and build a team with many people involved. I used the skills I had developed over the years to teach selling from a place of product knowledge, not sales pitches and empty promises. This served myself and the company very well, as profits were astronomical.

But soon that would come to an end, as the first big real estate crash of the 1990s would shroud both Merced and me with a dark curtain. We had bought our first home just before we married, improved it with a large capital infusion, and were soon upside down in our mortgage. Our jobs were both at risk. Merced's income dropped greatly, and my company decided to close the division that I co-managed.

Now it was time to get creative again and start another company of my own, specializing in alternative loan products. Now I had the experience with these types of loans and was willing to offer them up as a consumer-direct and wholesale product to mortgage brokers.

At this point we had not saved enough capital for me to go out on my own 100%, and so I partnered with an existing company and formed a new corporation. We became the first retail shop in the northern states to offer 100% financing on home loans! In fact, we were the test case for Wall Street in this newly created product offering. I wrote the guidelines, along with my head underwriter (my mother-in-law), that were to be used throughout the entire mortgage industry, soon to be securitized by Wall

Street firms and ultimately becoming a new asset class.

Within one year of successfully funding and selling these loans, Merced joined the team. She brought with her a unique style of management, experiential implementation of running a company, and systems for successfully originating, underwriting, funding, and selling loans. Together, along with various family members, we built an amazing well-run and profitable machine. Eventually we ran into some snags and disagreements with our partner. So, we decided to venture out on our own, as we had finally accumulated enough capital to do this ourselves.

Once we made the move to open our own company, we named it Nevis Funding, after the island in the West Indies called Nevis where we honeymooned. Once again, we created our own product line of alternative mortgages that were securitized and sold on Wall Street. Underwriting the loans ourselves, I personally prepared and sold the loans to the Wall Street investors, selling them in bulk just like big banks. Sometimes our loans were pooled together with multi-billion-dollar firms. We were a small player but were well respected throughout the entire mortgage industry. We traveled to Chicago for the Board and Trade, to New York to meet with the major Wall Street firms for securitization and loan sales meetings with corporate executives, and to trade shows to search for other firms to sell loans to.

All was going so well, as we had built up enough capital to sell the company and retire. But we could not just sell so easily, as we employed five family members, along with loyal employees that came along with us from past years. So, 2006 came around and we were notified that a possible temporary loan meltdown was coming and we should offer retail products only. This was a surprise to us, as we did not have any bad loans floating out there, and we were flummoxed at what was about to occur.

So, after six months of winding down our company, we stopped taking in any new loans from mortgage brokers and shut the doors in February of 2007.

I spent the next six months getting the rest of our closed loans sold, while Merced had job offers from various companies. She took a job as a direct lender with a retail mortgage company that was started by a friend. She would be doing construction loans and utilizing her skills to expand that division to new heights. While Merced was doing this, I was still pondering what I was to do.

We had an extremely high mortgage balance and payment and were dipping into our reserves to keep up with a monthly budget that we could not afford. We eventually sold our home at a loss, downsized our cars, and moved into a more affordable lifestyle. I was still searching for a new career identity and even considered waiting tables in order to keep some cash flow coming in on my part. This is where I really got creative and started brokering reverse mortgages, working for a close friend of mine who had been doing these types of loans for a few years. I studied up on this type of loans and realized they were a necessity for millions of older Americans with lots of home equity.

I would travel around to banks for leads, as most did not offer these types of loans. I also would call on mortgage brokers who were not familiar with these loans. I soon developed a steady flow of business that put me back in the game. Coming from the heights of my career to the lows of no income whatsoever and no identity, and writing out large-sum checks so that I could preserve my reputation in the mortgage banking industry, I finally had something to hang my hat on. This was what thrusted me forward into my current purpose in life, and that's taking care of our senior population.

Business Now

From the simple process of reverse mortgages, I once thought that all seniors aged at home, and that's where they would spend their dying days. Well, I was wrong, and now I discovered the world of assisted living and skilled nursing facilities.

At this point, I decided to start a new company which incorporated both reverse mortgages and assisted living. As seniors in America, you either age at home or somewhere else. That somewhere else is quite often at an assisted living community or a skilled nursing facility. So, I studied the Federal and State laws concerning both choices, took many courses, and am still on a continuing education path. I eventually became a Certified Senior Advisor, aka CSA®. I started my company The Life Planning Companies, specializing in the implementation of a true estate plan, which covers the legal, housing, financial, and health care parts of one's estate. We offer a systemic approach to properly aging in America called Later Life Planning®, and my goal is to have all Americans get Later Life Planning®.

Through my informative years, my hands-on sales years, the product development years, and times of adversity and re-birth, I have created something from nothing. Now I am looking towards a very bright future for myself, my family, and eventually all of America who use my system and services.

Having experienced adversity, stagnation, and self-worth issues, I have greatly benefited from these stages of self-awareness. I've turned challenges into learning tools and reached out for support from trustworthy family, ultimately succeeding on my purposeful path to personal success.

Chapter 5

Why am I here?
By Michele Cempaka

One sunny day as I sat amidst thousands of daisies that always emerged during the summertime, speckling the field at the back of our two story house, something magical occurred. I was only four years old, but I felt at one with nature and her majestic beauty as she gently enveloped me. I was told by a psychic that at this very moment, the angels smiled down upon me and chose to bestow the gifts of healing and psychic abilities upon me. What I didn't know then was how challenging this blessing would be for the rest of my life.

I believe that even before this day I had already signed up for my mission on earth. I have come here many times before to help humanity find freedom from suffering and to remember their true essence. Each time I incarnate on earth I must remember again why I have come here and what my mission is. It is not easy for me or any of us to learn our lessons and fulfill our missions which are usually fraught with many challenges. These challenges are actually our gifts, because they give us the opportunity to step into something greater and choose consciousness. Through our adversity we can learn how to be more tolerant and compassionate with other people and ourselves.

As a teenager I was often judged for my gifts and called a witch, because I had the ability to see someone's past, present and future. I thought this was normal, but I soon discovered that no one else had these abilities. Many people couldn't comprehend how I could know and do extraordinary things that seemed impossible for the average person.

When I was 15 years old we moved from Florida to Colorado because my father was laid off from his job. Unfortunately there were no engineering jobs in Florida at that time. I thought this could be a chance for a fresh start in a new school and completely different environment. I had high hopes that I might be more accepted by my peers and that I would finally belong.

When I entered grade 11, I quickly found out that my hopes and dreams for a better life would not be realized. Everyone had already established their clicks and close friendships from grade nine or even before in middle school. I was just an outsider who would be tolerated but nothing more. I no longer felt that oneness that I once experienced as a four year old girl who sat amidst a field of daisies. I was now resigned to the fact that I would never belong, because I was just too different from anyone else.

These repeated experiences of being rejected or betrayed by others in my life created my 'original wound'. We all carry our own original wounds which often derive from our childhood experiences. When we are willing to face our wounds and go into our buried emotions for just a little while, we are then able to fully heal ourselves from our traumas or painful experiences. If we instead choose to avoid dealing with our wounds, they will fester. When this occurs we can become deeply depressed or experience other kinds of emotional, spiritual, physical and mental issues. I think these painful experiences in my childhood led me into a very dark place. This is when I finally came face to face with the dark friend known as depression who stayed with me on and off until my late 30's.

"The wound is the place where the Light enters you." — Rumi

There is a vibrational frequency for every emotion we have. When we generate and feel love, gratitude, peace or joy, we attract more of these high vibrational energies to us. But when we are holding on to anger, fear, resentment, un-forgiveness, jealousy, etc, which are all lower vibrational frequencies, we ultimately attract experiences to us that hold the same vibration. The key is to discover any damaging emotions or thoughts from our past and present, that are being held within our bodies and cellular blueprints and release these. Once we do this we can live a more fulfilling and empowered life.

Spiritual crisis is our soul telling us we are not on track with our life mission

When I was 38 years old I experienced a spiritual crisis which catapulted me into another deep depression; I realized that my marriage was coming to an end. My son Danil was only three and a half years old. I was filled with guilt and confusion about whether to stay in my marriage and with a man who no longer had any desire to be intimate or even communicate with me. I had never felt so alone or rejected and I knew that if I didn't find the strength to leave, my Spirit would be deeply fractured. In Shamanism we call this 'Soul fragmentation'. This is when a person undergoes a deeply painful experience or traumatic event that is too overwhelming for her to face in that present moment, so she actually disassociates herself breaking off her consciousness; this soul fragment is then left in that time. In truth, I think my soul had already started to fracture.

My fight or flight mechanism kicked in and I chose to run away to Bali. I got a job as an online English language teacher which was very new and cutting edge at that time. I was amongst the first group of teachers to teach in a virtual classroom which was a totally foreign concept to me, as I knew very little about computers at that time. It turned out to be a really fun job which was just what I needed to help me offset the deep sadness I was feeling about my failed marriage.

Seven months later in October 2002, the Bali bombing occurred in Kuta. I was living in Sanur at the time and heard two blasts. My soon to be ex-husband had come to Bali to finalize our divorce. It all seemed so bizarrely synchronistic somehow that our marriage was ending and Bali got bombed at the same time. I went to work as usual but I couldn't concentrate. My students in our virtual classroom kept messaging me with chat to ask what was going on and whether I knew anyone who had gotten killed in the bombing? I didn't know what to say ... my hands felt heavy as I tried to type back a response. I couldn't do this. How could I sit here and teach a class knowing that many people had been killed or seriously injured? My hands stopped and then I slowly typed: "I'm sorry I can't teach you today. I need to go home now." I picked up my purse and looked at the other teachers who were still trying to teach their classes. A few of them stared at me with bewilderment as I said I had to go and walked out of the office.

The bomb was a metaphor for my life. It was telling me to wake up and step up but I didn't know how or what I was meant to do? One of my friends mentioned that there was a well known astrologer from Australia who had come to Bali to help anyone who needed guidance after the bombing. He was doing astrology readings in Ubud, so I booked an appointment in the hopes that he could point me in the right direction. I saw him at a table in the corner of the restaurant with his laptop open. I sat down beside him and he asked for my date and time of birth which he then used to generate my astrology chart. He asked me what I did for a living and I told him that I was an online English teacher.

He shook his head from side to side saying, "No, no, no that's not what you're meant to be doing."

"What do you mean?" I asked feeling confused.

"It's right here on your chart. Do you see?" he asked as he pointed to Kyron: an asteroid that represents the wounded healer. "You should be a spiritual counselor or healer."

I thought this guy had totally got everything screwed up. Maybe he had inputted the wrong birthday for me or time? There was no way I was meant to be a healer!

"No, that can't be right. You must have made a mistake?"

"I'm absolutely sure. Its right here," he said emphatically pointing at Kyron. "If you don't follow your true path, then you'll never be happy."

I was astounded by his words. I was convinced this guy was a fraud and had no idea about who I really was. I thanked him for the reading and made excuses that I needed to get back home. I was angry that I had spent $50 on his astrology report which was a lot of money for me at that time, as my salary was only around $600 a month. I had no more clarity about my next steps than before I had come to see him. In fact, I was probably more confused which angered me even more.

A Calling to Step into My Greatness

A seed had been planted deep into my subconscious by the astrologer's words. As the days passed I couldn't help but think about what he'd said. Somewhere deep within my being I knew that it was all true, but I had been in denial for many years. It had just been too painful to acknowledge who I really was – an empathic woman with the ability to heal others. I didn't feel ready to do this as I also knew that I still had a lot of my own self healing to do before I was ready to help anyone else. I felt there was so much more that I needed to learn about energy healing, so I joined a Reiki 2 class with a wonderful Reiki Master teacher named Cat Wheeler, who lives in Ubud. This level is where I learned how to send healing through time and space with the use of sacred symbols. I was especially attuned to use these symbols. A Reiki Master has the ability to directly channel these symbols from the Universe into the person she is attuning. In many ways the Reiki attunement is like a healing, because one's whole energetic system is activated and naturally realigns to these powerful energies, which gently enter our etheric field and travels to anywhere within our bodies that requires balancing or healing.

In 2007, Cat Wheeler invited me to join her Reiki Master training. This was the catalyst for a profound awakening that completely changed the course of my life. There was no turning back now even if I wanted to. Thus began the deconstruction of 'Michele' who I had known for over 40 years. I recall, just after the training, sitting down on our living room floor which bordered the garden. My stare fixated on a gray wall which was between our home and the neighbors. In that moment I had no idea who I was. I had been a practicing Buddhist for 12 years, but I no longer felt like a Buddhist. I had been brought up as an Episcopalian, but that conditioning had also miraculously fallen away. I realized that I no longer believed in any one religion or practice, because none of them were wrong or right, good or bad. It felt strange to let go of everything I once believed was significant in my life and just accept this 'nothingness' that was so foreign to me. I recalled the many times I'd repeated the 'Heart Sutra'. Every time I came to the line: "No eyes, no ears, no nose, no mouth, no mind." I had always stumbled on the 'no mind.' I never knew what that meant until that moment when everything fell away.

I began to hear voices in my head. For awhile I thought I was going crazy, but then I realized that my guides were talking to me – they had always been trying to reach me, but before I wasn't quite open enough to hear them. At first I was excited that my psychic abilities had become stronger as a result of being attuned as a Reiki Master. After a few weeks of not sleeping well because my guides were constantly communicating with me, I was exhausted. I didn't know how to get them to be quiet so I could get some sleep. I decided that I should go see a well known Balinese 'Healer' who lives in Singapadu, Bali. I had seen him a few times before for other physical issues which he had been successful in clearing up for me.

I arrived at his family compound and had to wait my turn, because there were a few other people waiting to get healing from him. Finally it was my turn and I stepped up on to his 'bale' – a small open pavilion and sat in front of him.

"What's wrong? You look like you're not sleeping well," he asked smiling revealing a broken tooth.

"That's why I'm here. My guides won't stop talking to me. I can't sleep. I'm exhausted! What should I do?"

"Just tell them you want to sleep now and they have to be quiet," he said laughing.

I felt like an idiot. "That's it? I just have to tell them to be quiet? Why didn't I think of that?"

He pressed hard on several points of my head and said, "You'll be fine now. Just tell them you're available during the day only and not at night when you need to sleep. Don't worry."

I went home feeling relieved but also slightly embarrassed that I didn't figure this out on my own. That night I did as he instructed and slept like a baby.

When we choose for the world our challenges get even harder

In 2014, I was invited to join a women's empowerment group which mostly met online. This had always been a dream of mine to come together with other like-minded, conscious women who truly desired to support and empower one another. I was sitting in a café with a lovely woman who was already in the group and we were talking about the possibility of me joining.

I paused for a moment and said, "Let me tune into myself and ask from that space."

There is a wonderful tool that I learned from Access Consciousness™ which is to ask:

"If I choose this what will my life be like in five years?" Then I waited to get the energy of that question, not the logical answer. It was feeling light so I went on.

"If I choose this what will my life be like in 10 years? 20 years?" The energy got even lighter so then I asked:

"If I choose to join this women's empowerment group what will the world be like in 10 years? 20 years? 50 years?"

Suddenly a huge wave of energy hit me and also made powerful contact with my friend who was sitting in front of me. We were both astonished by the intensity of this energy; I had my answer. I knew in that moment that my choice would actually be a contribution to the world. I felt so much joy in my heart and gave my friend a big hug. We were both laughing like school girls who had a juicy secret.

In the beginning it was such a beautiful and healing experience for me to be a part of this women's empowerment group. I felt for the first time in my life that I finally belonged. The women were strong and loving – they accepted me and each other and strived to create a safe space for every woman to share. As time went on the leader changed to someone new as this was the protocol. The new woman was very different from the other two leaders who were truly walking their talk.

Our new leader was scattered and pushy. When we tried to approach her and talk about how we felt about her leadership style, she became very defensive. Weeks passed and a tension grew between us which became very uncomfortable. I could feel that she had many entity attachments and offered to help her, but this only angered her more. What was once a safe refuge filled with light and love, had become heavy and disempowering not just for me but for other women who began leaving the group one by one. Another woman in the group that I didn't know very well had even confessed that she was afraid of our leader, because she knew that she had strong spiritual powers and thought she might use them against her in a negative way.

What is the gift of betrayal?

A few weeks later our leader told me she wanted me out of the group. She blamed me for all the problems the group was having and said it was my negative energy that was blocking the group from moving forward. I was totally gutted and felt completely betrayed. I couldn't believe this was happening. I felt totally disempowered and began to feel my original wound rising up again. How could I have been so wrong? I recalled that day when I'd felt such a powerful surge of energy which was my green light to join the empowerment group, but now everything was falling apart.

After our call, I sat down on my sofa feeling a deep despair. In that moment the energy waves powerfully thumped me like I've never experienced before; wave after wave of despair struck me in my heart center and flowed down the front of my body. This was beyond any feelings of depression or personal pain – I started to realize that I was feeling the collective despair of the all the women in the world who had been disempowered. I knew in that moment that I had agreed to facilitate this process for women everywhere, so that a new possibility of empowerment could be actualized for all of us. What I didn't know back on that fateful day when I asked those questions about what the world would be like if I chose to join the women's empowerment group, was that our choices for the world are not easy for us personally. In fact, they are often the toughest for us. My tears flowed down my cheeks and on to my chest as I cried for a very long time, for all of the women who had been bullied and betrayed. Kwan Yin had come to show me the despair that she transforms for everyone with her compassion and forgiveness.

It was not long after this experience that things took a turn for the worst. I was riding my motorbike home one night from a friend's anniversary party. A friend offered me to stay the night at her home, but since it wasn't too late and I only lived 30 minutes away, I politely declined saying that I preferred to go home. About 10 minutes from my house on a very dark road, a white dog suddenly appeared in front of my tire. There was no time to break or slow down. Everything happened within seconds as my bike crashed into the dog and I slid with my bike across the road. I remember laying there unable to move thinking "Is this it? I'm okay if it's time for me to go now. I've lived a good life." Then suddenly a voice boomed in my head, "No! It's not your time!" I knew then that this meant I would suffer as I could feel I was injured badly. Some Balinese men saw me and came rushing onto the road to pick me up. They carefully carried and lay me down on the ground speaking in Bahasa Indonesian. I was semi conscious so I couldn't comprehend or answer them at first. Finally I started to become more conscious and I was able to give them my husband's number. I asked them what happened to the white dog I hit. None of them saw the dog, which was a bit strange.

My right shoulder had a bad break and the doctor said I really needed surgery to repair the break properly. I refused and decided after three days to see a specialist. He told me that I didn't have to have surgery, but it was unlikely that my arm would heal perfectly without it. I knew that this was my opportunity to trust in my own healing abilities to heal myself, so I chose not to have the surgery. Instead every day I gave myself energy healing and took Chinese bone joining medicine.

It was excruciating to heal myself, as I could actually feel the bones moving back into place. After six weeks of healing myself, I decided it was time to get another x-ray to see the progress thus far. When the new doctor looked at my old x-ray, he said he would have absolutely advised me to get surgery. However, after looking at my new x-ray he was astounded by what he saw. My arm had nearly completely healed. There was only a thin gray line where the break once was and the bone that had been jutting out had moved back to its original place without any signs of being broken. He was totally perplexed as to how this could be. I just smiled and said, "Positive thinking." There were still many months of rehabilitating my muscles which had become quite stiff and weak from so many weeks of being restrained by a sling.

Several months later I did an exchange with a lovely woman who is a psychic reader. When I told her about my accident she looked at me and said, "That wasn't an accident. You know the woman who sent you that energy to kill you, but you are no longer in contact with her."

Her words struck me and in that moment I knew who she was referring to – it was the same woman who had bullied me and the other women in the Women's Empowerment group. A part of me was horrified to think that someone wanted to kill me. I felt anger rising within me as I asked, "Why did she do this?"

"You were a threat to her authority. She was not really holding the feminine energies of empowerment but instead was still stuck in the masculine energies of domination. Your role in this situation was to help her realize this and change it, but instead she chose not to."

I felt a profound sense of relief to know the truth of this whole situation that had occurred over one year affecting me and my family on so many levels, as I tried to navigate my way through the pain and confusion of what was occurring. A few months afterwards, I had another psychic reading from a man in New York who told me almost exactly the same thing, although I didn't reveal what the other psychic had said. Then a clairvoyant friend from the UK confirmed the same information. Now there were three psychics unbeknownst to one another who confirmed that this woman had tried to kill me. There was no longer doubt in my mind that this was totally true. I had to make a choice about what to do: 1. I could continue to hold on to my anger and unforgiveness. 2. I could let it all go and move forwards in my life. With time and more self healing, I eventually let go of my anger and forgave this woman who I knew was deeply in pain. I began to feel compassion for her suffering and realized that she had attacked me because I had come into her life so she could see her pain and deep seated anger and finally heal it. Just as she was a catalyst for me to truly be empowered and understand what true compassion is.

I have had several teachers from 2003 – 2016 that have had a profound impact on my life. However, my biggest learning has come from the challenges and adversity that have arisen in my life that I have faced and overcome. More and more I understand how all of these challenging experiences are actually gifts which have facilitated deep transformation and empowerment. With each challenge I have become stronger through my willingness to learn and grow from the lessons that life brings me.

Instead of closing down, which many of us want to do when faced with challenges, let's ask questions to help us understand how each difficulty in our lives has helped us rise higher and higher. It is incredible how life gives us exactly the lessons we need to expand our consciousness and open our hearts to truly become compassionate human beings. Every day I feel such gratitude for my life knowing that I can make a difference in the world with the work that I do facilitating consciousness and healing for myself and others.

If everyone knew that they were **Enough**, the world would be totally different. When we know we are Enough, we can truly be at peace and share that gift with others. Please remember that **You are Enough!** Write it everywhere in your home and it will become a positive imprint in your subconscious until you consciously know **You are Enough**. What energy, space and consciousness can your body and you be, that will allow you to open up to your greatness for all eternity?

Chapter 6

My Courageous Journey of Transformation
By Julie Kennedy

Life is filled with many challenging situations. As long as we're alive, we'll be confronted by challenges. Some will be minor tremors and some will be major life-altering crises that can erupt like a ferocious volcano and can rattle us to the depths of our core. Challenging situations or events are designed to bring us uneasiness, discouragement, frustration, and misery. If it weren't for challenges how would we grow emotionally, spiritually, and psychologically to reap the eventual gifts they provide? Challenging circumstances provide us with a story we can use to empower, motivate, and inspire others. Our testimony will be that it is possible to cope when the wheels fall off and our lives temporarily fall apart. It's how we respond to the challenge that makes the difference in the quality of life that we live.

We always have the freedom to choose how we move through our challenges. We can either grow from them or we can become a victim of them. For me, I discovered that the most difficult element to challenge was finding the courage to embrace my fear and work through the aftermath of the eruption, unsure of the outcome. Eventually, I learnt that by asking for help and opening my heart I was able to allow my vulnerability to have a voice. It was from this place that I was able to receive the benefits of the challenge. Courage, self-acceptance, connection, and faith are keys to overcoming our obstacles, and that's what is needed to reach the light at the end of the tunnel. The human spirit thrives on a meaningful connection. We are programmed to connect with each other, and one way to connect is through stories of how we have overcome life's adversities.

> *"Only those who will risk going too far can possibly find out how far one can go"*
>
> ~ *T. S. Eliot*

My life has been filled with challenges from the moment I exited my mother's womb. I seem to have experienced more than the usual of the life-altering volcanic-eruption crisis-styled ones; in fact, you may well refer to me as a Trauma Queen.

Throughout my teenage years and as a young woman I always carried around a feeling that something wasn't quite right. I used to have this inner unshakable feeling that something was wrong with me. I thought I was bad. I was fearful and infested with guilt and shame.

One day whilst walking home from school I remember becoming engulfed with a sense of knowing that I was more than what I was currently experiencing in my life. It felt like, somehow, I was somewhere else, or something else observing myself and my thoughts as I walked home that afternoon. I didn't really think too deeply about it at the time; I just accepted that this was a part of my life because it wasn't the first time I had experienced a presence and connection to something intangible. However, on this particular day, this presence was strong and wanted me to know that I wasn't walking this earth journey alone.

These experiences gave me a great sense of connection to something both inside and outside of myself. I would feel immense ease and peace; yet, simultaneously I felt a deep separation from this place. I ached and longed to be within that vibration, that realm which felt so near yet far, to be at one with this force continuously rather than momentarily. This place was familiar to me, and, within my heart and soul, I felt a deep connection to it. I believe it was my connection to this ethereal source that saved my life when I lost my way. It assisted me through my many challenges as I began awakening and remembering who I am and why I came here.

In the eighties, when I was in my early twenties, I was swanning around in the music scene. I was hanging out with local and international rock and pop stars. I had back stage access, attended exclusive parties, and had an inside view of the hedonistic lifestyle of the music culture of that time.

However, underneath my gregarious party girl exterior (one of my masks), I was struggling with an inner chaos of tumultuous anxiety which I would pacify with drugs and alcohol. I never knew at the time that this insidious energy I embodied was anxiety or why I had it. I just thought it was a part of me, a part that I didn't like, and I was willing to do anything to get rid of it. By the time I was twenty-five, things in my life were completely out of control. The wheels had well and truly fallen off. I knew that if I didn't get help and make serious changes I wouldn't be around much longer.

At this time, I was struggling with substance abuse, and I was trapped in a relationship with a man that I can only describe as a sociopathic narcissistic criminal. He had pursued me like a moth to a flame, filled with the desire to obtain me and bask in my light with the shadowy intention of extinguishing it. This man was violent and chillingly unpredictable. He was dangerous both psychologically and physically. I saw things that, for most, would be inconceivable and was forced to participate in acts that many would only ever be exposed to by a riveting psychological thriller on a screen.

He wasn't my first abusive relationship; I had been attracting abusive connections and relationships for some time. However, this relationship took me to the depths of my psyche's darkest crevices, where I found a darkness that was scarily powerful and seductive. By the time I realized it, I was embroiled in the precariously volatile underworld. I was in way over my head. I had become the classic naive victim, playing out my unconscious shadow parts in the severely dysfunctional labyrinth of the life I was caught up in.

I do not blame him for all of the events that happened in my life while I was in a relationship with him. Initially there was a part of me that found it quite exhilarating. I was seduced by the fantasy that finally I was being protected by a very powerful man and that I would be looked after. As you can see, I had also fallen victim to the entrenched disempowering delusional Cinderella vibe. Except, this fairytale involved some pretty serious players who were prepared to do whatever it took to rule the roost, and for some it didn't finish with a typical happy-ever-after. Now, you might be wondering why I thought I needed looking after and how I moved from sex, drugs, and rock 'n' roll to becoming ensconced in the destructive web of sex, drugs, violence, and criminality. Well, I can assure you from my own experience, the crossover veil was very thin.

Let me take you back in time and share a little more about my past—in particular, my early childhood—to gain some insight into how my journey started. I grew up in what psychology terms a dysfunctional family with an insecure attachment to my parents. This means, I never had a great connection with either of them. Growing up in this environment resulted in a significant impairment of my ability to form my identity and to feel valued. It left me feeling a deep sense of loss and separation. I never felt like I belonged or had the right to my voice. The lack of nurturing, protection, and structure from my family of origin contributed to my neediness in relationships. I lacked boundaries; I had a very limited sense of self and low self-worth. Therefore, I was an easy target for predators, as my unhinged childhood had made it easy for them to penetrate my loosely woven boundaries and wreak their havoc. However, the predators had truly been leaving their corrosive scarring well before my teenage years, as I would eventually discover.

The lack of family anchoring and the absence of connection with my parents left a deep void within me that I desperately wanted to fill. Self-medicating with drugs and alcohol had become another coping mechanism. Even though a part of me knew a life of substance abuse wasn't for me, at the time it was a part of my survival kit with which I'd seek comfort from the emptiness within and to silence my anxiety and the unbearable pain.

Now, my story so far may have been a different one if I had been raised with more love, connection, and support, but I wasn't. And, yes, I believe it's a parental responsibility to provide a safe and secure environment for a child to thrive. However, my parents did not provide such a safe environment, due to unresolved attachment styles and unprocessed trauma from their own childhoods. I discovered this much later when writing my thesis for my masters of counselling and psychotherapy, when I researched my family history across three generations. The purpose of this paper was to assert whether or not I had differentiated from my family's history across these three generations. I discovered a pattern of addiction, abuse, and dysfunction. Discovering this information helped me to accept my childhood on a deeper level. From previous self-developmental workshops and training, I had already realized that there was no point in blaming my parents for what had happened to me. Instead, I was working on becoming empowered and embracing the array of traits I had received by being raised by my parents: parents, who also were still desperately searching outside of themselves for love, acceptance, and belonging. Sadly, this was a major issue in the failure of their marriage.

Furthermore, my choice to take this perspective doesn't bypass my parents' responsibility and the part they played in my childhood. However, by learning how to forgive them and accepting this truth, I was able to embrace a freedom where I was no longer fighting, punishing, or resisting them or myself. Was I able to reach this place of acceptance easily? No, I wasn't! I was very angry, hurt, frustrated, resentful, and spiteful about this for many years. It really messed me up for a long time. However, instead of trying to keep up the pretense of all's-well and mask and deny my negative emotions, I learnt how to accept my volatile emotions and constructively employ them within my life. I also learnt how to regulate or discharge the more destructive ones.

I'm not into pseudo positivity pushing; I believe exaggerated positivism is a form of magical thinking that only creates more suffering. I let go of forcing myself to think positively when my truth was anger, frustration, sadness, or fear. The acceptance of negative emotion is a willingness to consider what is not working or acknowledging an imbalance in our lives. As I mentioned earlier, I was tired of punishing myself and wasting my energy on tearing myself down. So, I committed to doing the emotional work to heal the trauma that was keeping me stuck and impairing my ability to move on with my life. I committed to seeking out a more conscious way of being.

In my formative years, I unconsciously managed my anxiety, and the lack of connection and guidance in my life by becoming a dreamer and aloof. I have memories of continually staring out into space and losing time. I found myself fantasizing about being in other times and places. When I felt anxious, I would tune out, not listen, and at times isolate myself from others because I was so overwhelmed by guilt and shame. I embraced this self-soothing behavior with a tight grip like a child with her favorite blanket. I later discovered this was a coping mechanism called detachment. The problem was, I had no idea what I was detaching from.

My anxiety was intertwined throughout my body like a magnificent Moreton Bay Fig tree's root system veiled beneath the earth's surface. However, unlike the mighty fig tree, I wasn't being supported or thriving from the connection. Instead, I was being engulfed by it. I was bullied and got into fights during high school, which contributed to my relentless anxiety, but it wasn't the sole root cause of it.

Anxiety robbed me of many things and was a constant saboteur and driver of my destructive life choices. I had no awareness of why I felt fearful and anxious most of the time. I just did. I was locked inside my own internal prison. I felt uncomfortable in my body; my mind was often filled with frenzied ruminative looping thoughts that fear and anxiety feast on. I was disempowered. I longed to be loved and accepted; yet, I was needy, detached, and terrified of intimacy.

For years, I struggled with not feeling safe inside my own body. I'd never liked my body, and I fought myself over this. I always felt that something wasn't quite right with me. Yet, I couldn't work out what that something was. I hated the fact that whenever I was the center of attention I would be engulfed with anxiety. My heart would start racing, my neck and face would flush bright red, then the shame and guilt floodgates would burst wide open. By this stage, anxiety had hijacked me to the point of disorientation. All I could think about was how I could get away. My nervous system was constantly wired for high alert and prepared for danger.

I would often ask myself, "Why is this happening to me?" In time, I would discover that Why and a secret that was locked away deep within my cellular memory. That secret made me feel anxious and incredibly uncomfortable, especially when I was around men. I was doing whatever it took to keep that secret buried deep down there. Only, it had other ideas.

This skeleton in the closet was desperately trying to get my attention. It wanted to be seen, heard, and released. However, a part of me did not want that secret to surface. I wasn't ready to acknowledge it; I had no support at that time to deal with this intrusion. I thought it was best to keep it locked away, and every time it attempted to raise its ugly head I would simply push it back down by numbing myself out with substances. I was terrified of that secret; I didn't want to know about it. A part of me knew that, once the truth was out, there was no turning back, and that part of me also knew there was a lot of pain and suffering attached to this secret.

However, Spirit had a different plan for me. Spirit knew that my secret had to come out. So, I got thrown a shocking curveball where I was presented with an opportunity to change my destiny. I was being called to choose to either remain in victimhood or to radically change the course of my life.

This was a very difficult, chaotic, dark time for me. As I mentioned earlier, I was trapped in a relationship that had very limited options for getting out unscathed. Deep down, I knew I had to act on this curveball, as shocking as it was. Something inside of me knew it was my last chance to escape the turmoil that had become my life. I also knew my window of opportunity would be short: I could sense it like a snake senses its prey before striking. However, my way out involved risk, a huge risk, and once embarked upon there was no guarantee that I'd be safe. I decided to strike…

This was a turning point in my life. I was being given a second chance to turn my life around. Intuitively, I knew that I had to take it and that no matter how tough things were going to get—and things did get tough—somehow, I knew I would make it through this transition. It was time to disengage from the dense energy of this paradigm that I was functioning in. It was time for me to be courageous, to cultivate blind faith, to listen to my intuition, and to trust the unknown. I decided to trust my gut on this one, and it was right. And so, I managed to successfully escape the clutches of this dangerous man but not the psychological wounds that had been etched deep within my psyche, wounds that would need healing for the sake of my sanity.

However, I packed this trauma away just like my secret. I decided it best to put a lid on it and screw it down extra tight. I made the decision to move on with my life because I had been blessed with a second chance, and guilt and shame told me I'd better suck it up and make the most of it. I enrolled in art school and lied to myself about my past and my fragile emotional state.

By the second year of art school, the cracks were starting to show and I knew I needed help. I was emotionally breaking down. I had to admit to myself that I needed help. It wasn't easy for me to do that, as I was in denial about the severity of the damage my traumatic past had caused. I was ashamed, and a part of me thought I probably deserved it because, after all, I believed that somehow I was innately bad.

My secret was starting to gain more traction. It was time to peel another layer off. I had reached a place where I wasn't able to keep the lid on tight anymore. I couldn't keep on functioning this way. The pain was becoming unbearable. I had hit another wall and was starting to self-medicate with alcohol. I was scared, but I was tired of battling myself, and, for my well-being and sanity, it was time to get some long overdue help.

So, once again, I summoned my courage and sought out my first therapist. Fortunately, I was guided to a spiritually orientated therapist who could see me and hold space for me to feel safe as I started to unscrew the lid. It was from here that I was able to allow the immense grief and pain to begin to emerge. This was the start of my journey of transformation, remembering, and awakening. Later, I joined a women's group and participated in self-developmental workshops, all of which helped me in my quest in the unpacking of me.

However, something still didn't feel right.

At the age of thirty-one, I experienced the traumatic natural birth of my first son, an undiagnosed and complicated breach birth. I was again engulfed with sadness and started to feel uneasy. My relationship wasn't that great, and it was becoming unnervingly obvious that I had attracted another abusive partner. He was a heavy drinker, controlling, and verbally abusive. Even though I had begun my healing journey, I was hit with the realization that I still had a long way to go, and my inner secret was persistent in making itself known. Then, one day, I was flicking through a spiritual magazine when I came across an ad for training in a healing process called Rebirthing. I was instantly drawn to the image of the woman who was staring out at me from the page. I knew I had to do it. I booked in.

It was during an eye-to-eye breathing process that I was confronted with a series of colored visual images of my secret. Finally, my secret had been revealed, but I didn't want to believe it. I told myself it was ridiculous: I'd obviously made it up. So, I decided I would not accept what I saw until I asked my mother about the visions in the images. When I told my mother of my experience and what I had recalled she said, "Yes, you did go over to that house to play on the boat, and I believe that probably happened to you." I was speechless. My insidious secret was out and confirmed. I had been sexually abused by my father's friend, and, worst of all, my mother had suspected it may have been happening.

In these visual memories, I recalled the sexual abuse that I'd experienced from a friend of my father's when I was about 8 years old. These traumatic memories were repressed, I believe, because of the alcohol I was given before the abuse. This vital piece of the puzzle was like the domino effect. In my mind, I visualized all of the other dominos falling, one by one, representing the sequence of events that had shaped my life due to that experience. At first, I was bewildered by the deep effect that this repressed trauma had, had on my subconscious and the amount of damage that it had caused in my life. For example, the alcohol I was given before the abuse set up an unconscious pattern of promiscuous sexual behavior that I allowed in my life for quite some time. That pattern played out like this: when I would meet men in social situations and they bought me drinks, I would usually end up going home with them to have sex. These encounters were soul-destroying. This dysfunctional behavior only affirmed my underlying corrosive core beliefs that were fueling my anxiety.

Just before my son turned two, I left his father. After trying couples counselling, I could see there was not going to be a happy-ever-after once again. Due to the repression of this event, at that time, I had no conscious awareness of the energetic pattern that I was embodying. This pattern was transmitting a victim vibration and predators were easily able to latch on to it and weave their way through my loosely fabricated boundaries. It was still some time after the revelation of my sexual abuse before I would cease emanating this damaged vibration.

After completing a Vipassana retreat in my mid thirties, I gained more insight into the toxic programming I embodied in regard to sex and intimacy. In light of this, I decided to embark on a year or so of celibacy. The relationship I entered after my celibacy was an immensely enlightening one. It was through this relationship that I learned the implication and effect of cellular memory. My learning came via the cellular sensory system. My discovery came via touch. I was repulsed by this man's touch at times: it made my skin crawl and literally sickened me. Intellectually, I had already begun to understand the implications of cellular memory via my breathwork training. However, I had had no conscious visceral experience of it until then. It was a major ah-ha moment when I realized my body-mind system was being held hostage from my past sexual abuse. It was influencing my relationships and impairing my decision-making. I was making choices based on my faulty unconscious programming from my past abuse! I was blown away when I connected the dots on this one.

Additionally, this dysfunctional patterning had been affecting my body-mind system for years, and it had begun to break down. I had become chronically ill about five or so years earlier. Just over a year ago, I was formally diagnosed with a disease called fibromuscular dysplasia in my renal arteries. In March of this year, I suffered a blood clot in my left kidney. I thought I might die. To be honest, a part of me wanted to die—a part that has been trying to die for quite some time. This deeply wounded part of me that was filled with rage, shame, blame, guilt, and resentment had to die in order for me to fully awaken and remember who I am and why I am here.

Since my blood clot, I have reconnected to Source and my spiritual guides. I had packed all of that woo-woo stuff away some years earlier. I had decided to deny my connection to other realms, as it seemed the easiest thing to do at the time. I chose to hide my gifts like I'd been hiding my pain. I can no longer do that. I am at my best when I tune into the magnificent vibration of the multi-dimensional consciousness. It was from this place that I was able to heal my kidney, which was nearly 40% damaged from the blood clot I had suffered. My doctors were surprised to see that my kidney had healed by 90% when they received the visual imagining a few weeks after the initial clot took place.

There have been many key elements that assisted me in my healing journey. However, for the purpose of this chapter, I'm going to focus on the three significant ones, namely, courage, self-acceptance, and connection.

Courage

"You gain strength, courage, and confidence by every experience in which you really stop to look fear in the face. You are able to say to yourself, 'I lived through this horror. I can take the next thing that comes along.'" ~ Eleanor Roosevelt

It takes courage to recover and heal from trauma. Courage builds strength, confidence, and resilience: skills which are necessary to make the changes in life that lead to a safer and more secure place. It takes courage to get in touch with and meet the painful feelings connected to the unbearable memories of trauma, shame, and loss. Courage gives life. Courage sets boundaries. Courage has enabled me to overcome my fear and give me the strength to face my pain and grief. Courage has taught me to be open, honest, and truthful with myself and how I express my feelings. Courage enabled me to crack wide open when I felt broken and not be afraid to reach out and ask for help. This was a major first step for me on my healing journey.

Courage taught me to challenge my toxic beliefs and thoughts instead of falling victim to them. Courage taught me to push through them and not become stuck in the relentless ruminating loop of self-judgment, fear, and overthinking my every move. Courage gave me the strength to reach deep within my heart and share my truth regardless of my fear of rejection and abandonment. Fear has the power to take your life away if you let it. My past suffering has been an opportunity for me to cultivate and express my courage. By facing my pain head-on with courage, the path ahead appeared before me and the light that materialized showed me the way.

Self-Acceptance

"You don't need to be accepted by others. You need to accept yourself"

~ Thich Nhat Hanh

Self-acceptance didn't come easily for me. As I've mentioned, I was cloaked in guilt and shame about my past for many years. The difficulties of my early childhood left me feeling unworthy, ambivalent, and confused. I took on the belief that most of my behaviors were unacceptable. In many ways, I came to see myself as inadequate. I berated, blamed, chastised, and punished myself for what had happened to me and saw myself as defective. I suffered the I'm-not-good-enough virus for many years and internalized the many painful feelings of rejection, abandonment, and judgment. Throughout the years, I continually beat myself up.

So, how did I become more self-accepting?

I sought help and shared my pain. We aren't meant do it alone. I stopped punishing and blaming myself. I stopped denying, judging, and rejecting myself. I started to accept that, given my circumstances, I did the best I could at the time, just like my parents did. I started to trust. I started to release the exaggerated guilt and shame. I let go of the insidiously destructive self-criticisms. I let go of believing I was unworthy of love. I let go of conditions and conditioning. Instead, I opened my heart and became a channel for my own healing process by cultivating courage, compassion, understanding, and forgiveness for myself and for others.

I embraced my darkness and started to make peace with all the parts of my fragmented damaged self. Owning, integrating, and accepting all my various facets—the good, the bad, and the downright ugly—has truly been a transcendent experience. It's crucial to embrace an attitude of forgiveness for our transgressions, regardless of whether they're actual or perceived. For me, evolving to a state of unconditional self-acceptance is an ongoing process, like mindfulness: the more you practice it, the more you embody it.

Connection

"We're hardwired for connection. There's no arguing with the bioscience. But we can want it so badly we're trying to hot-wire it." ~ *Brene Brown*

The above quote fits perfectly with my past pursuit of connection. I wanted connection so badly that I was hot-wiring my system for it until my whole structure eventually broke down. I so desperately wanted to connect with others that I would literally sacrifice my Self to fit in and be accepted at all costs. I would attract and pursue deadly relationships that only bought confirmation of my toxic core belief of unworthiness. I was desperately searching for a sense of belonging, a sense of identity, a sense of security. I craved to feel safe, loved, and supported, to be part of a loving, functional environment. Yet, all I was connecting to and attracting was more abuse and pain.

Once I started my healing journey of processing and integrating my trauma I discovered that underneath the vortex of unworthiness and anxiety there was a Self that wanted to be birthed. An innocent pure Self that was buried deep down, entangled in all the toxic shame and guilt of my past. I noticed that, even though I wasn't who I thought I was, or who I could have been, there were some really good things about who I had become. Trauma had changed me and I didn't feel safe to, or even know how to, let this Self out to become who she wanted to be at the time.

It was momentous in my recovery process when I stopped searching outside of myself for belonging and acceptance and discovered how to deeply connect with my Self. When I learned how to truly accept, love, and honor myself for whom I'd been and who I was becoming, I started to drop the body armor and embrace and connect with who I wanted to be. Once I committed to this, I noticed that I started to attract experiences that allowed me to explore, discover, and embody the elements that made me feel connected to that part of me. When I accepted that I was responsible for my own fulfillment and reconnected to my core source, I shifted from powerless to powerful. It is from here that I have been able to reconnect to my deepest, truest self, where I can come from a place of love, authenticity, and grace.

****

"Take chances, make mistakes. That's how you grow. Pain nourishes your courage. You have to fail in order to practice being brave." ~ Mary Tyler Moore

I have journeyed far and deep to reach this destination of freedom. I spent years searching outside of myself, playing an unconscious partner in my victimization, hoping my emptiness would be fulfilled by another. This will never happen. I have made mistakes, taken risks and failed. I've ventured into the darkness, the craziness, and the cesspit of life. Some days were so unbearable that I thought I wouldn't make it, but I did! I made a choice to live a new way of life, to embody a new container. I took responsibility to deeply connect, love, and honor myself, no matter what, rather than expecting someone else to do it for me. I've finally arrived at a place where I am no longer a victim of my past.

I am a living testimony that trauma can be transformed, that bodies, minds, and hearts can be healed. Addiction can be overcome, and love can be healthy. My journey of trauma was not a path that I had expected to travel, but, rather than allowing it to devour me or continue to hide from it, I now accept it and own it. My story by no means is intended to negate the severity and the long-term damage, consequences, and effects of sexual, verbal, or physical abuse. This is my own personal story of my courageous journey of transformation, healing, and triumph to date.

Chapter 7

Thriving, My Way
Authenticity does not always come easily
By Trish Rock

That day, when my client showed up, was the day that changed everything.

The change

As humans, we change moment by moment, without even realising it, until one day we arrive at a place where we do not even recognise ourselves. This is evolution. It is slow. It is precise and it is a natural part of who we are.

But when we *consciously and deliberately* decide to make changes in our lives and ourselves, that little voice of fear rises up and often stops us in our tracks.

Quite often the biggest changes to come to fruition are the ones that involve us being our authentic selves. Why is that so challenging? We are born being our truth, our self, our human, and our spirit energy. And then, somewhere along the timeline of life, we forget, we are taught otherwise, we stray away from our Truth and we get lost in it all.

~~~~~

Back in 2008-2009, things were starting to shift for me in a bigger way, an obvious way. I had been cruising along in the fingernail industry and, after many years of being in business, I decided to take it to a home-based salon. I was over the push of it all. I was done with the stress and expansion, constantly needing to be more in order to have a place in the town.

I had left the industry before this, just before the breakdown of my second marriage, and for eight years was in property management. But when the stress of that began affecting my health, I went back to what I knew in my bones. The nail industry had always been the easy road for me. Yes, there were challenges, but I was really good at the skill, always managed to be booked six months ahead, and never had to worry about money coming in.

But something inside me was calling out, was crying out, for change.

Change of a different sort.

You see in the years previous, I had been divorced for the second time, had built my first home and had to sell it in the settlement, and then went on to buying, renovating and selling two other properties until I bought the one where I placed my salon.

Things were actually going really well! On the outside and in the physical human sense, that is.

On the inside, I was dying. And I blamed everyone around me. Again! I seemed to have a habit of this: never taking responsibility for how I was feeling and choosing to change it. (But I did not realise it until 2012. More on that later.)

It's interesting that the challenges of divorce, property investment, life, business and bringing up an extended family, which were big challenges to many of my clients, were never as great for me as the challenge of being uniquely me.

This day, in 2009, a client arrived at my home salon.

The epiphany

That moment when we get it is one we never forget. It may just happen once in your lifetime or several times, but I think that the more stubborn we are in the process of change, the bigger the ah-ha moments are. It's like we bang our heads against the wall for so long (I call this the flat forehead syndrome) that it's only when we take that last approach to the wall and finally *see* that moving forward again will mean more of the same—another bang to the forehead—that we finally stop, breathe, and change direction.

~~~~~

A fortnight earlier, this client at my salon who had come for her next visit had asked me some questions about her life and wondered if I had any solutions. I was always very good at this. From the age of 17 when I began in the Industry, it always came very easily to me, giving advice on any topic and always leaving my clients feeling like they had a solution. I feel this was one of the biggest reasons my salons were always full, as the experience I offered people was different to other salons.

I was never clear on exactly what this was that I did. I thought I simply had good people skills, which I do, but this was a different level.

The appointment that day made everything so clear.

The client sat down and I asked her how everything was and specifically about what we had spoken of at the last appointment. (I was also very good at remembering the conversations I had with every single client even up to 10 per day.) She proceeded to tell me that after her last visit she decided to go to a psychic and get some advice. As she began to relate what the psychic had said to her, it dawned on me that it was exactly what I had told her.

Then it hit me. I knew what I had been doing my whole life. I could offer solutions to people, the same as a psychic could! I still was unclear about it all, but I knew that this was what my soul had been trying to show me for quite some time. I think sometimes we have to be at a very low point to actually see or hear the messages we are given! But they are there always without having to hit the low.

At first, I was angry that she had not listened to my advice. I felt undervalued. I felt invalidated. I felt like a lowly nail technician with no worth except to fix a broken nail and paint it red.

Of course most of the people who came to me were not going to take what I advised them seriously. They were there to have their nails done, not have a psychic reading. And although they all felt better for some reason after a visit with me, the conversation was taken at that level, a conversation, not a soul to soul communion, which it was.

I had a bigger message and this was not my audience anymore.

So, becoming clear on this truly freed me from the grip of another downward spiral of not feeling valued or important in this business or in life.

As humans we can really get caught up in what society deems as the right thing. Often this game we play leads us to feeling very empty on the inside, and even when we appear to have it all—husband, good life, house, car, money, whatever it is for you—we can actually not have peace and joy. Real peace and joy, I mean. And this is when the alignment of who we are is out of balance and we feel de-pressed. Unable to rise into our unique energy. Unable to rise into our true Being. Unable to just be ourselves.

Often the challenge is in not even knowing that this is why we are spiralling!

It was a short time later that I decided to change my life.

My daughter was off to University at the end of 2009, my son had already set up a life for himself in Canberra, and my step children had gone their own ways. What was actually keeping me here in this physical and mental no man's land?

Nothing.

So, I made the decision to sell the business and the house and move somewhere new. The idea was to get away from all the things and people that were making me miserable and to start again. I was going to find a source of income far removed from the nail industry where I could earn money from home online. I was very done with face-to-face clients by this stage in life. I would build finances and work towards the business where I would be the person who gave unique advice to people intuitively.

Yes, my plan seemed good!

And the greatest challenge of my life so far began.

The road to finding myself

Once we make the decision to change, the road is not always clear. I've always said, though, especially to my clients that have been caught in the fear of the new road ahead so much that they cannot make the decision to go through with any changes, that the most difficult and challenging part is the decision itself.

The decision for any type of change can take years. But once the decision is made, everything then seems to go along with more ease and certainly more speed! The path becomes clear day by day and, with the pressure of the decision out of the way, we are back in that emotion of wonder: wonder for all the new things coming and the magic that starts to take place.

~~~~~

It felt so good being in a town where no one knew me, where I could do my own thing, learn new things, and feel free to be me.

I had never really felt at home for the 16 years I spent in Queensland. After I moved from Canberra and sold my salon (my baby!), I seemed to have lost some of my passion for life and business. I blamed my marriage, and I blamed the town. I blamed the clients. I blamed my children. I blamed the Universe.

I thought that, if I could start again in a different town, with a different business, different people, and new conversation around me, my happiness level would increase and I could truly be the joyful person that was authentically me.

But wiping the slate clean is not the answer for internal happiness, so I discovered. There in my new home by myself, with no one to blame for anything I felt, I was still unhappy.

And so it started: the search for myself.

After seeing me post on social media that I had lost myself and was now working to find myself again, someone asked, "How do you know you are lost and where did you go?"

I thought that was a great question!

How did I know I was lost? And where DID I go?

I went down the path of not showing up as my unique self. Yes we all do it. Yes, sometimes we realise it, and other times we don't. The status quo is a comfortable place for many humans.

Social media became a lovely outlet for me at this time in 2010. Interestingly enough, in 2009 when I started on Facebook (begrudgingly, as I thought it was just a bunch of school kids bitching about each other!) I didn't understand its value to people personally and also generally.

For me, it became a beautiful place where I could speak my truth to an audience that wasn't really there in front of me to criticise, condemn, or judge. I understood that I could get a lot of bad feedback through this media, but for me this was less scary and confronting that speaking the truth of who I was to people in real life.

I began to write various messages I was receiving, and when I look back on those early posts, they still ring true and for me. This is a great gift of understanding: when we come from that authentic heartspace, the words we speak and write will never lose their energy and meaning.

I was finally feeling like the real me was standing proud and becoming louder.

But then there were the challenges of business.

My roadmap didn't exist yet

As we carve out a new path for ourselves in life, there are no roadmaps. It is all trial and error. I think the most important thing to remember, and what I have learned the most from this challenging journey, is that it is vital to listen to your inner voice and your innermost gut feelings.

Your innate knowing must come before any other short-term, short-lived, or shallow victories.

Doing something just because it earns you good money will mean your soul will not be fulfilled and you will feel trapped and lost. One big thing I have come away with from the past nine-year cycle is that, yes, money is great and we need it; yes, money can provide a lot of freedom in life; and, yes, money certainly can bring happiness. But ALL of this must begin within you FIRST. Otherwise the money will not fill those desires of joy, love, freedom, and inner peace.

My roadmap began with a huge barrier to creating money: a business that worked and a lifestyle I loved.

~~~~~

Bingo!

After a whole lifetime in a business that I knew and that came easily to me, where money flowed and where I was mostly validated daily, my challenge now was to start something new, something I had to learn, something that was not yet bringing in daily money and which certainly was not bringing me any validation!

But I kept on. The first business attempt left me feeling cold and unemotional. And even though I loved all of the technical stuff, it was not floating my boat. I could not see myself doing this for a long period of time.

It really was a case of, "This will make you money so just do it the way we are and it will work." The trouble was, it wasn't me. I didn't connect. It didn't resonate and I didn't want to earn money that way.

Since I still had some savings left, I wasn't in a panic over it.

I moved on to the next recommendation of a career that seemed suitable. Reluctant at first, I entered back into the nail business but this time as a Global Coach. This enabled me to apply the techy skills I was learning and I could also help people I related to in a way they understood.

Working this way opened up a whole side of life that had not even been in my mind or imagination a few years before! This is what change will do. Letting go of the old makes space for the new.

There was a lot of exciting stuff that happened in this period of time. I wrote a few books. I did my first two-hour business talk and got paid, too. I also wrote my first paid workshop and travelled to other states to deliver it.

I discovered that I could actually talk about the things that excited me, such as spirituality, authenticity, and self-love and self-worth, wrapped up in useful information that helped people to run more profitable salon businesses. It was fun!

The financial side of this was very challenging, however, and I was in an industry that did not have a lot of money. I was too stubborn back then (and intimidated) to expand into the hair and beauty field where there was more scope for greater rewards.

Looking back now, I can see that there was a lot of resistance around money, which was preventing it from coming in. But at the time I thought it was my lack of skills and that perhaps I was just too stupid to run any other business than a simple little nail salon.

Over the following years, I was almost tempted every now and then to simply set up shop and do nails again. It would be the easy way out for me.

But my soul knew differently and was drip-feeding me the vision of the greater me. It was all I could believe, in little bits. If I had the grand vision then that I have today, it would have scared the bejesus out of me!

So, in its wisdom, and in the energy allowance that was running through me then, little by little, Spirit helped me to see my challenges as part of the grand design, and I started to embrace them. Spirit also showed me what I was capable of, too, and I learned so many amazing things!

So, as I dived into each attempt at bringing in an income so that I could support my work in getting a bigger message to the world (the irony of it all is comical as I write this), I felt more and more stupid, more and more unworthy, and to be honest I really didn't think I was good enough to succeed at anything else except the nail industry. This tortured me and kept me in a depressed state, which, of course, did not help with the business building.

If it hadn't been for some very special friends and mentors over this time, people who carefully pulled me from this self-hatred and loved me deeply, I'm not sure I would have surfaced from it. Or it would have taken me a very long time.

Over the years I've had to get various jobs to support me while building a business. So, rather than hating these work-for-money jobs, which I had to do as I attempted to build a business so I could go spread my message, (There it is again! The hilarious irony of it all!) I embraced the challenge in this way: I found a way to incorporate my bigger vision into what I was doing.

A great example of this was when I was working at an RSL club (Returned and Services League). I got the job as the promotions person, bar attendant, and Bingo caller (Yeah, I know, right!). It was actually a fun job, but in the beginning I was terribly down on myself for ending up here when I wasn't smart enough to be earning money from my own business. I was surrounded by people who had beautiful hearts but really couldn't see past the daily life they were in. Maybe they had had dreams once, and it all got too hard. Who knows? But I didn't enjoy the conversation, the energy, or the mood of it all.

Once I stopped with the victim mindset and realised I could actually feel joy and happiness no matter where I was or what I was doing, I saw the amazing opportunity the Universe had delivered to me.

So, at this workplace, I then decided to learn what I could to help me in my bigger vision. I used it as the next stepping stone.

One of the things I did was to be deliberately happy. In an environment where people were not happy with their jobs or lives, this caused many people to not like my happiness, the Happiness Police, as I called them: those who didn't like others to be joyful, because they were not joyful themselves and didn't know how to be.

I was always laughing and giggling, and so many people actually started seeking me out. My energy lifted them. It healed them. I loved that. I especially loved how it helped, lifted, and healed some of the regulars at the club who were very lonely and came for the company. They certainly enjoyed the banter and giggles!

I discovered that there were many opportunities here in this job where I could learn things that would serve my higher purpose and vision:

•Talking with people about their lives and learning about humanity;

•Learning different practical skills within the job as well as the promotions, raffles, and the bingo—all fabulous jobs to learn my microphone skills in front of a crowd;

•Honing my stage skills.

While calling Bingo, I decided to practise my stage skills and microphone skills, as part of my bigger vision was to be speaking from stage. So, as I called the numbers, I would project my voice into the microphone as if there were 5,000 people in the room who had come to see me and hear my message: straight back, great stage presence, hold the microphone with confidence and poise... "17, one seven...88, double eight...36, three six..."

No one except me knew all of this going on behind the number-calling, of course. But it felt good for me and I was enthusiastic about the work I was doing. The challenge of having to earn money this way was made easier.

In between games, I would write down all the ideas I had for my book, my programs, any articles etc. (I found one of the old bingo sheets a little while ago and saw the ideas I had jotted down. Some were already a reality.)

The challenge at the time was to somehow enjoy and be grateful for the job that was bringing me income and not to be focussed on the disappointment and sadness that my failing business was bringing me. That, and certainly to stop feeling that I was not good enough.

Being a victim to all of the things that were not working was not helping me at all. I got called out in a very public way on this in 2012, and I was just starting to truly understand what that meant.

Victim mindset

None of us are victims of life, even though many of us feel this way throughout our lives.

Why is it that we choose to believe others are in control of our lives, our destinies, our feelings, and our freedom? Why do we find it so challenging to accept the responsibility of everything in our lives?

I feel for many of us it is a pattern that starts when we are young. Trouble is, by the time we have been in this mindset for umpteen years, we can't see it as a mindset; we see it as natural and a part of who we are.

But it is not who we are.

It took many years for me to figure it out and remember.

~~~~~

Early in the adventure of my new journey, I was in Thailand, where I was learning web-based technology and design. It was an exciting time for me. Also, I hadn't travelled much up to that date, and going overseas was amazing!

The people were lovely, the classes were great, and I had a lovely experience overall while I was there.

But the biggest thing to come out of it, on a personal level, was the change, or beginning of change, to my mindset and behaviour. I truly had been wallowing in my own self pity most of the time. Yes, MOST of the time. The worst thing was that I wasn't even aware of it.

Here is what happens to us as humans, no matter what mindset we have: we usually all gather together—same mindset with same mindset—and we all speak the same language and enjoy the same story.

I'd become used to being around others with a victim mindset, too. That's why it didn't feel out of place. We could all gather together and complain about everything: all the terrible things life was throwing at us; all the people who were causing us to be angry, mad, upset; or any other emotion we chose to use at the time.

The sad thing is, while we are in that mindset, even the fabulous feelings we have, like love or happiness, we also give the responsibility to another.

Thinking like this means we have no self-empowerment at all.

Needless to say, we didn't know this. Of course, it was everyone else's fault! What are you talking about? Of course, they are to blame!

That night, on that trip, everything started to change.

I found myself in a group of people who were not victims, and after a little while they got sick of hearing all the blame and whining coming from my direction. And one of them called me on it.

"If you are going to stay a victim here in this situation, then I'm walking away. I'm not interested in hearing it. You can change it if you choose to."

Whoa...

And with that, she walked away. And so did the others, leaving me there by myself in a place I did not know, in a country I did not know. I tell you, it really hit me hard. But it didn't stop me from the drama, not at first.

This experience has always stuck with me. I remember it to this day. I felt like crap.

That was a defining moment in my life. It was very challenging, and still is, but it helped me turn the corner to the path that was calling me.

In the bigger vision I had, there would be no room for playing victim.

The people who get ahead in this lifetime are self-empowered and CHOOSE how they feel, react, and act.

There was a challenging path ahead of me, but I knew it was time. I had to focus on the bigger version of myself to help me ditch the smaller one. It was time to start, and I'm truly grateful for the person who called me out of the shadows of my own self-sabotage and drama.

Big Vision

Do you have a big vision? Can you see yourself in a totally different space, mind, and experience than you are currently living?

It's more than money, this grander version and vision of ourselves. It's truly about serving our purpose here. Stepping into that picture of ourselves that we know we are and delivering our Divine message to others, in whatever form that takes.

For you it may be fame. For another it may be relationships. Someone else may want to climb the career ladder to serve well. And, for another, their message may be in the love and nurture of their family.

We all have purpose here in this lifetime and in the living of Joy in each day we find it.

We also require a bigger vision, or goal, to help us leap or to crawl, ever so slowly, over those hurdles that are in our way.

It is so easy to give up. With every challenge that comes along, we have the choice: face it or don't. But without good reason to go through the emotional and mental growth pains, many of us stay where we are and live life, as is, because we believe, "That's my lot in life anyway!"

But what if we didn't?

~~~~~

I keep having this vision.

I am on stage, with thousands of people there who have come to see and hear me. I feel I have helped them all in some way and that they have come to be even more inspired this night.

My family and loved ones are in the front row feeling very proud.

I don't know right now exactly what I am speaking about but I am not nervous up there. In fact, I feel quite at home!

This vision has kept me going through many a challenge.

I have pushed through some of the smaller challenges with reasonable ease, like the job mindset I adopted. That not only helped me in the moment with earning money through jobs, but it also helped me with business failures. My mindset here is, there are no such things as failures, only effort and the next step forward.

During the four years or so that I truly was stuck in poverty mindset, I knew, in my essence, that there was a lesson here, that there was something here that I was going to benefit from, that there was something here that others were going to benefit from.

This didn't help the situation at first though.

All I did was complain and complain, forever the victim even though I was making an effort NOT to be the victim.

Lack mindset can be overpowering in some respects.

When I was being coached and guided to see beyond what was in my bank account and remain within a positive, abundant perspective, it truly was challenging daily when more bills than income came in, when money kept going out. And on those days when I truly didn't know how I would get by! How could I FEEL abundant when I had less than zero to my name?

It was a very long slog, I have to say! And I honestly did not understand it at the time.

I have been successful since the age of 24. I had dragged myself out of near drug addiction, the pension, two divorces, and no lustre for life to a business I loved and was great at. Money was never an issue really.

So, why now, after 28 years of abundance, was I struggling to stay afloat?

I actually got further and further into self-hatred for a while during this period, and the apparent failure of a few businesses dug me in even deeper.

Then things started to turn, and it truly was my big vision in the background of my thoughts that kept the Light at the end of the tunnel for me.

And the Light also consisted of the beautiful people around me at the time. Earth angels. People who never gave up on me. People who could see the bigger picture that I couldn't see yet. People who held me up when I wanted to fall.

I think it was at this point, after nearly four years, that I truly began to see the abundance all around me.

A beautiful soul friend, who always had my back no matter what, taught me so much about life, about abundance, about love, about myself. My fears of letting her down were always rebutted with the notion that that could never happen. What a blessing she was in my life and heart.

Always knowing the perfect thing to say or give, this beautiful friend also gifted me one day with a book that shifted a lot for me. A book by John Kehoe called *Quantum Warrior- A Future of the Mind*. In this book, I found a lot of truth and could see a different way of being, I also remember specifically that moment where in it he described a time when he had no money and had to live on grapes for a week.

This blew my mind because I could totally relate to it! There were weeks (or more) when I had to be clever with my resources, too, so that my dogs could be fed and myself. It wasn't always easy. This gave me a renewed sense of okay-ness. Maybe everything was going to be all right.

My boyfriend at the time, who also saw me through the eyes of Light and Love, was always lifting, always mirroring my Light. He was a true blessing I will never forget.

At that time, I also had another Earth Angel friend who had such deep kindness and strength for which I will always be incredibly grateful.

Among other things and at different times, there was once when I couldn't pay my rent. Despite working my business and a job, I still had no money for rent. This particular day I remember so well. I was beaten. Done. Didn't feel I could rise again.

She came to visit and while I kept these things to myself she knew instinctively that something was wrong. To cut a long story short, she gave me a week's rent so I would not get kicked out of the house. That in itself blew me away, but here is what floored me:

This money was ALL she had for herself. And she offered it to me.

This one act, on top of the beautiful and unconditional love I received from her and my other soul family, truly brought me to my senses about abundance.

The challenge was over in a way.

I now understood that we can feel abundant in every moment. And when we do, we are.

There were so many amazing moments and people in my life, and I wasn't recognising it. All I was focused on was the lack, the struggle, the pain, the failure.

My vision became clearer, and I knew at that point that my time in poverty had taught me many lessons. Why did it have to last so long? Because the greater the struggle the bigger the message we have to teach. That vision of me on stage truly has gotten me over so many challenges.

I now also knew that I would be helping others with abundance. What a blessing!

After that time, I looked at every daily struggle with grace and gratitude: Learning to teach, teaching to learn.

Sometimes (actually always!) our challenges are experiences that allow us to truly be able to share how we overcame them and to encourage others to do the same. I knew the four previous years and the ones to follow were just a part of the jigsaw and it was all coming together to allow me to deliver a much bigger message.

I help a lot of clients with this shift in perception, too, and when they can see that their troubles, struggles, and challenges are actually truly helping them in some way, the resistance lessens and the abundance channels flow once more, in all ways.

Soon after this, when life moved me, supported me, and presented me with many other opportunities to grow and expand, I realised that one of the things that had held me back (of my own doing and beliefs and no one else's) was not Being myself, in my style, in my way, with my energy.

I finally got it.

To thrive, rather than survive: it was up to me to shine MY light, not a version of another's.

Thriving, My Way

We only have to look to nature to see that uniqueness is a standard and the norm.

We don't see a daffodil trying to be a gumtree. We don't see a kangaroo trying to be a whale. And we don't see any other plant or animal attempting to be anything other than what it is.

So why as a human are we always comparing ourselves to others? Why do we go to great lengths to look like another? To act like another?

Why is it in business that we are often taught that the formula that served another well is what we must do to succeed, and then when it doesn't, the only variable is ourselves?

Just like nature, we must BE ourselves to thrive. And we must also be aware that to thrive is also as unique as we are and no one can dictate what that means.

I knew what I loved to do. I knew my bigger vision. So why was I not thriving?

I had to take a big long look at my life.

Why was it that my salon businesses were successful for so many years with little effort—it didn't feel like effort!—yet the massive effort I was throwing into these other businesses was not paying off financially yet?

I truly did not understand it, but I got out of the victim and pity mode and decided to really look at this quandary. Then it occurred to me!

When I was in my salons, I was me, in all ways. I walked a path of my own making, was not a follower, was not mimicking anyone, and was not following anyone else's road to success.

It made total sense finally!

I understood, and I went about changing things.

And the first thing I changed was my abundant mindset. One of my gorgeous girlfriends helped me with this and I couldn't be more grateful. In our first session we decided that my money life sector was the most pressing and needed work.

My question: What would you actually buy if you had the money you were seeking?

This seriously changed so much for me! I couldn't think of anything. And there lay the problem. If you don't know what you want the money for, how can it come to you? And I'm not talking about bills. I'm talking dreams, desires, wants, and the just-because.

My abundance energy kicked in and after a few weeks I had actually written 100 things that I would buy. It wasn't easy! But I did it and got the flow started again.

You see, this was the total opposite of lack mindset where all I focussed on what I didn't have.

I was now focused on what I COULD have and what I wanted in my life.

There were still many challenges to overcome, but without the victim mindset things became easier.

At the beginning of this year, 2017, I decided to look at this scenario:

What do I Love to do?

How do I love to do it?

Being that, Being me

What came of it? Well I got back to the mentality that I had when I ran my first salon.

What do I really love doing and how do I love doing it? It all seemed so simple really!

Now I have to say that the training, coaching, and mentoring over the years that preceded this did not go to waste and were very relevant. I still use a lot of it. The change was that I started to use what I needed in a way that served my energy.

You see, we all have unique energy and when we attempt to be, do, or behave like another person who may have been successful or happy or whatever it was that attracted them to us, we lose our true identities and soul vibrations in what we do.

It is actually our unique light that attracts others. Yes, we can use business models and follow what others are doing or have done, but in all relationships in this life, including business, people are attracted to our energy. Get those elements flowing and there is no push or struggle. Just pure joy for every daily step while growing and expanding.

I often wonder why it took me so long to understand this, especially since I'd written a book about how to attract people into your business! Just another one of those life challenges that forces us to truly look at how we are showing up.

And here is the best learning: while my salon business was successful for those 28 years, my skills with money were not at all good. The challenges over the past seven to eight years have truly allowed me to not only adopt a beautiful abundant mindset but also to learn about money, love it, honour it, and respect it so that now when it comes to me it has somewhere important to be, go, and do. The Universe sends me more now. It likes vision and planning.

Thriving, my way, comes easily. And it will come easily for you, too, if you allow it. I think sometimes the challenge with this is the learned behaviour of boundaries, the right things to do and be, and the pressure we have on us as society looks to us for conformity.

It is killing our souls, though, and we are starting to feel it. The challenge of Being uniquely YOU shouldn't be a challenge. It comes naturally to you. Well, it used to. Take time to get back to YOU. Remember how brilliantly perfect you are. Remember that gorgeous energy that attracts people to you. Remember your ability to be in flow. Authenticity does not always come easily, and for many of us, it takes great adversity and challenge.

It's how you react to the challenge that will determine the length of time you are in it. A new perception is needed. And it is time. Thrive now. Your way.

Love and blessings to you and may you have the courage to shine brightly.

Chapter 8

The Journey of Recovery
By Alexandra Calamel

How I happened to be in the Tsunami, December 23 2004. My mother, bless her soul, after not speaking to me for over 10 years sent word she was dying and her wish was to meet my family. A proud Dutch French women with a linage of Tall Ships traders off the Ivory Coast of Africa, from her father, who took runaway slaves to establish themselves in Rodrigues located on the border of Mauritius in the Indian ocean.

I was living in Queensland at the time, collaborating and selling Aboriginal Art in a Gallery on Mt Tamborine, getting ready to go to Belize. In Belize was a project, with Eric Ericsson the saxophone player, to build a retreat for creative souls; well you can see where I choose to be. Life happens and taking responsibility fully for my actions has always been my motto from an early age. I guess it comes from my mother's carefree spirit of drama wherever she went.

The journey continues as I connected with mums' family, to fly to Mauritius first and then catch a small plane to Rodrigues. I made my decisions quickly and synchronicity was on my side as I manage to get a lower price to go on my trip. I was leaving the second week of December for Mauritius, most people pre-booked their tickets months in advanced, especially in the Christmas season. The universe provides when you are on the right track for new experiences and even to a major disaster...lol. I wonder at times, is our life pre-planned to a written script and can we change all the scripts put in place.

I arrived at Mauritius Airport on 19 Dec 2014 to a scenery of flowing mountains and greenery, my next thought was, 'I am in a surrealistic exotic world of picture postcards, awesome'. My cousin had arranged her cousins to take care of me for a week and then on a small charter for Rodrigues. My interaction in Mauritius was of course family and also meeting with my older sister, that is another story in itself and for another book. The time arrived quickly for me to leave for Rodrigues even with cancelations and being left waiting for 12 hours at the airport until the next flight. I had a picturesque backdrop, eye candy, and the workers at the airport were the most gracious people I have met on my trip. The workers on the ground were taking care of me, keeping me safe and bringing food for me to have before my late flight of 10pm. A memorable time that shows a person can create their environment no matter what the circumstances.

The arrival on the island of Rodrigues was muggy and dark with another half hour drive to the house. All I could think of was that I needed a shower and sleep, then when daylight breaks to sneak out in the early morning light under a tree or on a beach to recharge. The morning came with the exotic-ness of most island life, the view of mango trees from the window, kids playing and neighbours chatting by your window, wanting to see the stranger from Australia.

Louise's daughter I am called, like a servant from a far away land where no one knew I vaguely existed. I am the youngest of 5 and no one really knew anything about me as my mother kept me a secret. I feel it's more her secret mistake, she made up and told vagarious vulgar story of who I was for the drama queen that she was. Please don't get me wrong I loved my mother, that's all I know as family but the lies, deceit of stories she told to her family and to her children about me was a novel in itself. My mother was the biggest BBB out of Texas (big, bold, brazen), for me it was the conditioning I needed for my growth and being kept away from my siblings is now the greater blessing of synchronicity after her death on Dec 23 2014.

The story continues with an unforeseen pallet of colours for the future stories I am sharing with you today. Back to the Island of Rodrigues, it is completely flat with one mountain in the middle and surrounded by beautiful reefs. Just like watching a documentary, I saw myself watching the scenery unfold at every turn from the tropical weather, the palm trees, the market on the beach front and the music coming from an Islam mosque… as you do. The locals are a foundation from eight families that settled there in the early 18th century, my grandfather was one of those families. He was a Dutch French trader up and down the Ivory Coast trading tobacco, tea and livestock. The other tall ships were French and one was even a red Indian; I found awesome stories. A large percentage of settlers were freed, runaway slaves that settled in Rodrigues on the plantations and merged with French, African creoles, Indian and Asian descendant, what an eclectic diversity of cultures living in a very small island community.

I spend my days seeing people, going to the port and bus rides to my mother's family. In my spare times I went down the beach meditating and just enjoyed the scenery. One of those days, on 23 Dec, I was down at the beach on the most beautiful day with a clear blue sky. The time was 9.00am and I thought I'd lie down in a secluded spot to meditate.

As soon as I took some deep breaths I heard my name called out. I have another name that I was given a long ago from the ether, I don't get to airy fairy with it as it is what it is. The name Fushiastar was toning in the wind, like a deep whooshing sound that went right to the core of my being. I opened my eyes straight away, stood up and looked over at the reef and smiled at what just happened, I hadn't heard my name being called in a long time.

I noticed that my intuition kicked in and I looked over to the reef and the voices in my head showed me that the reef had been broken. Surely not I thought as to the right of me was the lookout for such things and they would have sounded the siren by now. As I had been listening to my inner knowing for a long time, I wasn't about to dismiss what happened and proceeded to go back to the house on higher ground, which takes about 15min. I walked back thinking that my intuition never really leads me astray and a peacefulness of emptiness overwhelmed me.

I climbed those 30 steps to the house and stayed in the silence that overwhelmed my being in the moment and I felt blessed. There were 2 grandchildren that loved to spend time with me everywhere, within minutes I heard loud voices down the bottom of the stairs and among the mango trees. Now many people from the houses on high ground had come out to see what the commotion was about. The stories started to pore in as the water, at this stage, was at the bottom of the carved rock stairs. Many people were frantic and started to go and find out what was happening, from within myself I was stunned about what just happened.

The children with me, being kids, were already out down the stairs into the street and as I was looking after them I had to follow. In the main street, the water was already covering it as endless waves were crashing and sweeping across it. The water came in at fast intervals with people aligning themselves in shock of what to do. Since being on an island, everything was flat all around and living close to the foreshores anyone could see how high the waves were coming in and dragging everything away. I held those children hands tight as they wanted to follow their grandpa. By this stage I was on the main road observing. It amazed me how many people froze in fear or went closer to the water rather than going away from the disaster happening.

In the mist of all the commotion of people on the street and by the water, cars had stopped, people speaking loud to each other, some just stood there in shock. I was silent in a quiet space that I have never felt before. Within minutes I found mum's cousins literally in my face screaming at me of 'Why are you not upset with this happening and why are you so calm'? What can I say to a person that is in shock; nothing but hold my space and speak softly. At this stage I changed the subject to the kids. I have these 2 children with me, I have to take them to safety, I walked away back to the house, with the kids objecting. By this stage I was still pretty peaceful asking myself am I in shock or am I in peace but I wasn't about to analyse anything. I needed to get to safety with the kids, to higher ground and leave any other problems, whatever they were, later is later.

The aftermath was the salt water had gone everywhere due to a flatness of the island, between the banana plantations with the crops and shops on the water front sweep out to sea with the fish. No one was hurt or died, just the devastation of the waves on the island and the residents routines, it was a shock for everyone. The news in Rodrigues that afternoon showed where it started and the devastation that it took in its path and also we saw the amount of people that died, that day on television and for the next few days that followed. The water settled and I rang Australia at 12 noon and said 'Guess what I am alive' being the joker that I am. My friend said yeah we can see that, you are talking to me.

I continue to say I am alive from the Tsunami and everyone else on the island was in shock and not understanding what I was talking about. I proceeded to tell them what had happened and what the news was bringing forth; where and how many people have died at this point. There was no information on the news that day in Queensland Australia, I was told that in the evening on SBS there was a few minutes but not much said or shown. In my own country most people didn't hear anything about the Tsunami or talked about until the following week, amazing. The following days past Christmas was mainly the cleanup and people talking to each other more about the happenings. In the first week in Jan 2005 I was back in Queensland on Mt Tamborine.

Arriving back home to Australia was a blessing as I was safe and I had a place to go back to where I had friends that were really my family. The weeks that followed, coming back adjusting to the time difference, I didn't think much about it apart from been tired. Little did I know that I would be on a roller coaster ride of ill health, an emotional roller coaster and body breakdown.

The coming weeks felt like some other person took over my body with destructive tendencies, an emotional roller coaster, bleeding leaving me exhausted, and the craziness of non-connection of thought processes from my right to left brain. My thinking and doing things in the same way wasn't happening from my old self to that moment in time. The desperate search to focus was not connecting, the structures of everyday went out the window, the discipline nonexistent and the meditation, well how can you focus if you can't remember what to do. My creative processes went out the window even to the point of creating and saving a file on the computer then I couldn't remember where I put things and would have to do another file.

Within the cycle of all things in life there is a season, one for the birth and one for the death of Transformation. My story continues into a bubble of shock and nightmare, I call it 'what the' moments. In the following weeks I was exhausted, my breathing was shallow, walking became a struggle, food sensitivity had worsened and all I wanted to do was hide from the world and from my overwhelming feelings of sensitivity in every moment.

Living on the mountain is far from having lots of people like in the city and with my heightened awareness I could sense peoples thoughts, emotional pressures, I would even know when mobile phones would ring. I felt as if life became unbearable. Wow, my boundaries and filters to view the World were blown away, whooossshhhh.

It sounds great to have a good clean out of your 'structures of perceptions of what you think you are' but this was ridiculous. Boundaries are there to protect us and filters are there for learning experiences as we grow into this world of controlled learning, otherwise our senses would be blown away and you would not be able to cope.

My anxiety and overwhelmingness of living every day and not sleeping well took a hold of me. I made a decision to go back to Melbourne where I could find previous teachers I could connect to. Within a month of being back in Australia I made the big move from Queensland back to Melbourne, a large part of me was very happy. A friend of mine decided to follow me and we rented a house together close to things so I could go to doctors and get to teachers with alternative therapies.

The following 3 month I decided to get tested for everything. The doctor was very obliging as she saw how I had become with my weight loss and being grey looking. The people that knew me as being alive and chirpy saw I was becoming a recluse and not wanting to talk to or see anyone. If there was a cave I would have gone in it. I was not the same person that was the life of the party and made everyone laugh when in their presence, by that stage I evolved into the opposite.

The roller coaster ride begins as my body became tired, like I was an old women of 90 years of age, with minimal eating and drinking, all I wanted to do was sleep and be away from people. My time spent indoors was mainly with my friend that came from Queensland with me, he worked though and I stayed home. The doctors just put my condition down to the stress of being in the Tsunami; my stress level had broken down my immune system.

Going through a monthly women cycle was one thing, bleeding every week was making my iron levels low and resulted in a lack of clarity and dizzy spells, just to name a few symptoms. The doctor's suggestion, a full hysterectomy to stop the bleeding. After a year I said no. I went about finding other alternative therapies from teachers I knew previously but nothing worked, I felt helpless like I was trapped in a vacuum while my body was going through all these symptoms. I was getting better within my mindset and forcing myself to function with my every day routine, which is training and business and to also do something that was outside of my usual routine.

****

My new neighbour had children, during that time those kids saved me from boredom with play, art, storytelling and making beaded necklaces, simple everyday fun. With this little interaction with the children my neighbour decided to share with other mothers how I helped her special skilled children and many others then came for guidance. With that awesome offset I was repeating to myself so many times that I created the situation; 11 children, interactive with their parent, for special oversensitive kids.

When I was unable to do anything from the back and join pains that followed from being in a vortex of feeling old, I manage to look at computer graphics. I previously had no connection to the computer let alone comprehend what I was doing. I managed to create Mandala's as my Artwork. I used pictures I took of selected friends and numbers that would randomly appear in my mind; presto I would utilise PaintShop Pro to create Mandela's. I was not fully aware how to use the program in my state but in an altered state of not knowing it worked well. Even to this day I look at the screen dumfounded at what I am looking at and where do I go from there.

My mind opened within an area never before seen in my life and this has expanded many possibilities; to see and sense people even more. I managed to do some artwork that was way out there as I had never painted before. The symbols and waves of colour related to what was happening on the planet from an energetic flow; little did I know at the time. Even though I was aware, I did things without knowing, from within me, which was different for me as I came from a linear time of goal setting and training.

As I was getting better, years down the tract, I did some work with disability and advanced illness, all the while hiding what was happening to me, still struggling with my own health issues. Even though I had my own challenges I was still doing something part time within the parameters of what my body would allow me to do.

Then the piece de resistance hit me, my stomach was swelling and within weeks I looked like I was 30 weeks pregnant, just like my neighbour next door. Well there was nowhere to go but surrender to the doctors. One look at me and within a week he scheduled an operation, I was not impressed with it at all, as previously things were put down to my weak immune system. I was thinking of the things I went through since I came back to Australia. Between the tests, poking around and not to mentioned being in hospital for over a week for observation as I was coughing up blood. All this, I thought, after taking care of myself well over the years; from eating the right food and exercising, having a strong immune system most my life time and a kick in my step.

Now this 'What The' moment approached me with a slap across the face again and this time left me crying with thoughts of not wanting to be here. In

2010 within a month of the doctors looking at me I was on the operation table. I went in to remove the cyst and whatever was attached to it. I was a wonderful case study of a quick rush to the operation and a candidate to die on the table due to my low iron levels and my other health issues. Before the procedure I had to sign the paperwork waiving any negligence in case I died on the table. The lady in question said to me 'you do realise we have to find an anaesthetist to do this that is prepared to be there in case something happened'. She followed by saying 'as for myself, and 3 others I know, we will not take your case on and I feel one of the younger girls maybe willing, I will get back to you'.

The weeks that followed the operation to remove the cyst were long, waiting in case it was cancerous. All I thought through this time was this is just another day on planet body earth space. You also have to realise I didn't have family for support through this manifesto. I had my friend, that was a male, and he knew all the things that were happening but I did not want to burden anyone else. Silence of what was and what could be for change was my friend of keeping myself safe and sane in this dilemma of surrendering my body to an operation.

The operation came and the damage left behind from the cutting of the cyst that attached to various organs was phenomenal with a long cut to my abdomen that got stapled back to keep the wound closed. The extensiveness of the procedure should have left me in the hospital a minimum 8 to 14 days as the attachment of the cyst was extensive to most inner body parts. Within a day I was bright eyed and bushy tailed, the second day I wanted to go home as I didn't want to be strapped to a hospital bed.

A physio lady was called to talk to me about the extensive cutting and damage to the nerves inside me, that affected areas like the inner thigh, my sexuality, the bladder, and numbness was expected for a more than a year. She spoke to me how most people in my condition would not be up and about on the second day and she would not see anyone in this condition until the 5th or 6th day for exercise to strengthen the inner core muscles. All I could think of was get me out of this hospital and in my own home to heal. On the third day they reluctantly discharged me from hospital. With my persuasion they agreed a nurse or doctor would see me at home if anything happened.

I was home again, safe and ready for the healing process without being poked around. I found, while having a shower, bruises on my chest, in the next couple days my dreams revealed why. When I woke up after the operation there was a man and a women in black suits and writing pads visiting me. I thought it was odd at the time as they kept on asking me if I was ok. I didn't think much of it at the time as surely I wasn't that special, unless they found an alien inside me…lol. I soon remembered being out of my body and the paddle bruising on my chest, even though I signed 'do not resuscitate', confirmed what I was seeing.

A couple days at home I settled into routine. One morning when going to the toilet, the staples popped open, about half a dozen just under my belly button all the way down. I thought how can I move without bleeding let alone my inside falling out. Funny now, not so funny at the time. I managed to ring the doctor to come that evening to patch me up. As you can see, I'm still here sharing except I still have the wonderful scares on my body.

****

The biggest thing for me has been acceptance to making peace when going through the rough patches of health during this period. With all that could go wrong, in an instant happened, an experience that led to my biggest challenge. I was supper fit but was thrown left field of my good health and wellbeing and my body was not responding to what I was telling it to do.

Being dyslexic and ADD I learnt skills along my journey to function better in my life. With the Tsunami it threw all my pathways out the window and I was left with a scrambling mindset making it hard to function every day. I would see a picture but couldn't find the words to go with it and sentences were very confused. I felt like I was two people and so I slowly began the journey of functioning from one side of the brain to the other side. Relearning how to function with the basics of being in the moment and accepting where I was at rather than thinking of where I have been. Every day was a challenge to breathe, to walk and to speak sentences.

Taking a day at a time and not forgetting to fight when people said you can't Alex or you won't be able to do this or that with your health. I realised the very thing I lacked I needed to heal through the challenges. I had to fully let go of control and accept all that was happening, even though at times kicking and screaming with tears. All necessary to let go and unfold more energy within me and allowing more within to come out, even to this day.

During this period my creative side unfolded more than ever before. There was an amazing download of information that arranged themselves into stories and more. I have always been creative in my life and with my background of training and business I thought I was well rounded. I even did artwork of abstract landscape, dimensions of symbols of Melchizedek and graphics of core Star Mandela's that related to balancing the right and left brain. All this creativity was assisting with my healing process and being creative is a big part of my life even to this day.

The most profound messages I got from within me was through spending time in four walls having a great deal of patience with myself and allowing the flow of the cycle that was at hand. I had to stop my mind from forcing me from the old pattern of doing to the new and accepting, with less pushing to make things happen. Flowing during this time that I had no control over was a huge leap for me, as I have been an over doer and creator and chaser in business, in sports and health to perfection.

Three key points that helped me through my personal change

1. Having a background in meditation and Martial art assists me a great deal with the chaos of nothing working, by staying calm in those moments. With the knowledge of various modalities of meditation that I also knew I learnt to simplify my skills to achieve stillness, to go within myself. This also helps with any pain and frustration in my everyday life.

Being able to center and being in the moment is the ultimate gift I gave to myself.

2. My harsh conditioning from my mother gave me the patience of whatever happens to flow with it and finding another way to deal with any situation. Within my past conditioning of not been good enough, no matter what my mother threw at me all my life, right up to 2 months before she passed away, the patience I learnt pulled me through this time… to sharing this with you today.

3. Having a holistic approach to living life from an early age, I was able to apply that to myself in those hard times of my health deteriorating after the shock waves of the Tsunami. Having many skills allowed me to work on myself and keep my mind busy in other ways. Although I was weak, I began to create space within me that started to create art and stories from my busy past and restrictions.

It's always been a passion to write one day, well that day came and it took me going through a Tsunami to write Stories and children books. Please note I would not suggest that anyone find a Tsunami to go through to become a creative soul…lol. For me, whatever the reason was to go through what I did, I have no regrets and this only leads me to sharing my story with you.

WOW, the learning from pain, suffering and the frustrations leading to the simplification of living in the moment more! I am fully healed in most area of body, beautiful and functioning as I should be at this point, as a healthy human. During this last 5 and a half years I have also assisted 6 developing communities to create self-sufficient projects with Arts, which has been very fulfilling.

Out of left field I was also accepted to Melbourne University for a Masters in Art and Community Practices for 2017. Who would have known this was possible, coming from a dyslexic person that failed English all through high school and was told she was never going to succeed. Although the offer was great I decided to start my own practice using the advance techniques that I had been utilising on myself and others along my journey.

The skills that came through this process have been extraordinary and I gained greater clarity. For this reason I created a platform where Individuals can tackle their personal list of 'I CAN'T to their list of 'I CAN'.

Living my life up to this point has been with no regrets even with the hard times but it was balanced with exceptional times and wonderful people that I have met from all over the Globe.

In life we all have been through so many challenges to just be alive in this moment. I don't see myself different or exceptional, I see my life up to this point as living life to the fullest and what's around the corner is just another ride, whoossshhhh. I wonder what's next on this ride on Planet Earth.

Since this journey of discovery about my full potential as a human experience, life has been less challenging in growth with little steps moving forward toward my future. I soon regained many of my skills and they unfolded even better than before. Along this journey I studied and managed to do many things that led me to this point of my new horizon and a change to sharing with others what I have learn along the journey of living life to the fullest. At 54 my life is just beginning in a new way from my Can't list of my past to my I CAN list of choices and possibilities in 2017 and beyond.

Chapter 9

My Journey to Spiritual Awakening
By Ganga Dev

The beginning

Where did my path to spiritual awakening actually begin? Well I guess I could say that the actual beginning was growing up on Kangaroo Island, a medium sized island off the south coast of central Australia. I was fortunate enough to spend my first seventeen years growing up on a two and a half thousand acre mixed farm, in a somewhat isolated rural community of eight other farms and a lighthouse station. The farm was bounded by a national park to the south of the farm and massive cliffs leading to a treacherous coast line to our north and west. Amazing sunsets abounded and beautiful star lit nights as the milky way filled into totality, the night sky.

I had a knowing and a sense at such an early stage that I was one with everything yet separate at the same time. Often with my friends on a "sleep out" under the Milky Way we would try to comprehend the enormity of the universe and the knowing that it was boundless, whatever that meant to our pre-pubescent minds.

I used to do all the rural country things like working on the farm, hunting and fishing, playing games and sport, generally leading a life devoid of any stress whatsoever.

It was bliss.

Though being a farm boy I was very aware of the cycle of life; birth, death and renewal, through the seasonal changes and the management of the animals. Caring for them, managing their wellbeing and then shipping them off to be slaughtered for human consumption. It was what we did! That was the cold hard fact of farming life. I would always make observations of the animals, (we had sheep and beef cattle) and was intrigued by what I perceived was their social structure. The sheep had it, and so too did the cattle, though my observation was that the cattle were more, I suppose, sentient. Let me give some examples of what I observed on the farm.

With the sheep, I had noticed that when in a mob they would often be driven by the mob mentality and fear (as they were often being chased by working dogs and people yelling and making loud noises to scare them into complying to our wishes). However when observed on their own without any human harassment they would often do amazing things. They would play, especially the young lambs and would often play in groups. The mothers would always be on the lookout for their offspring knowing where they were and keeping an eye out for intruders. When walking I noticed that some sheep would always walk with their head down, yet others would hold their heads high and some would hold their heads in a neutral position neither high or low. I noted that as the sheep crossed paths some would bow to others yet to another group they would raise their heads up. My observations also revealed to me that the sheep with heads high often appeared to be the stronger more vibrant individuals regardless of their age.

We also had hand reared a pet goat "Rocky" who we then set free to roam with the sheep. He was an amazing animal. All the sheep would follow him when he was with the mob, in fact he would lead them into the shearing shed and they would dutifully follow him. Rocky would then jump the pens coming out of the shed to lead more back in. He would often step between the powerful male Rams when fighting (which was often to the point of physical surrender and sometimes death). He would observe them fighting for a period of time then when things looked like getting serious he would position himself between the two fighting animals and they would just turn and walk away as if nothing had ever happened.

Rocky was obviously the "Zen" master of the sheep! Though what was apparent to me was Rocky had displayed a high level of intelligence and ability to make choices, to actually help others live with less stress, it was an amazing thing to behold.

We sometimes hand reared orphaned animals, though normally they would be killed for meat. I had hand reared an orphaned bull (male) calf. He grew into a fine specimen of his species and was a powerful and beautiful beast. He always remembered me, and would often approach me as a grown beast for a rub of his forehead or even a suckle of my hand, however when he was in a paddock where other cattle could been seen he would never approach or respond to me in any way. Yet again a display of another decision or choice from these supposedly unintelligent animals.

Another example of intelligence, reasoning and choice was a beautiful breeder cow "#75" who would follow the farm tractor and trailer when we were giving out baled hay during the summer months (a nutritional necessity during lean months). She would follow right to the very end to where the last biscuit of hay had been tossed from the trailer, often taking the biscuit of hay directly from my hands. She would then feast on the abundance of fresh hay that lay before her as she worked her way back to the thronging herd who were fighting for position to get just a mouthful of hay from the others. "#75" had four offspring, all females, that she taught this technique to. They never fought or struggled to have their fill and were always serene and composed.

How did this life growing up on the farm affect my spiritual awakening? Mostly it showed me (as the universe so often does) that what we are told is truth is often very far from what actually is.

I learned and had great appreciation for the sacredness of all things and that indeed we are all connected in some sense or way.

Then I left the farm and was exposed to human societal life and basically "ran amok" for a number of years, learning about relationships, parenthood, work, sex, drugs and rock and roll! All the usual things that western youth often involves itself with, but always there would be a correction that would bring me back to the understanding that there is something more, something greater than what appeared to be.

In my late twenties, whilst on a self imposed six month rehab from my excesses in life, I discovered energy healing and learnt how to help others, and myself. Utilizing Great Spirit or universal divine energy, colour prana (energy) and discovering how to connect into all sorts of animate and inanimate objects often becoming one with that which I connected with. Through this time I luckily learned about and was able to practice invocation for protection and guidance. I learned of spiritual guides, light beings, how to utilize light (consciousness) for healing and protection and had become a sponge for all that I could learn about the new metaphysics and way of being, of reincarnation, soul mates, soul family, twin souls, and it all just made perfect sense to me.

"For those who are believers, no proof is required. For those who are doubters and sceptics no amount of proof is enough" and I was a believer!

Yet still I was not happy in life or peaceful within, I did have moments of lucidity and peace within having fathered three beautiful children and being involved with their lives and all that parenting brings, but was always searching, always yearning for the answer to life. In essence I was looking for the "Holy Grail" the "magic wand" that would fix all my woes and failings, fix all my past indiscretions. I wanted it easy, I didn't really want to work for it, I'd already worked hard enough!! Or so I thought.

By the time I had reached my mid forty's life had become very dark for me. My latest marriage had failed (it was my forth) and I suffered a heart attack at the ripe ol' age of forty-seven, from what I termed was a broken heart! I was not overweight nor had I high blood pressure or high cholesterol. Cardio vascular disease did not run in my family and I was quite physically fit for my age. I simply put it down to the fact that I had a broken heart. The medical profession did not agree and blamed the stresses of my business and that I had been a smoker in my early years (though no doubt a contributing factor).

Now most people when faced with their own mortality often experience an epiphany regarding their current situation and life direction, I alas was not one of those people. I became very angry and bitter towards life (this observation of course is from a position of hind sight) and buried myself in work and for one period of eighteen months worked every day straight excluding Christmas day! My two youngest beautiful children left home as soon as they were able, and I became more desperate for the "Holy grail / Magic wand". It was during this period of searching and feverishly spending my health insurance payout that I became a seminar junky!! Who said I had an addictive personality?

The middle

We have all heard the saying no doubt that the Divine moves in mysterious ways? Well I was just beginning to really understand, and identify this fact in my current life. It was during one seminar that a light bulb went off in my consciousness…I realised that I had just heard the truth, well the truth for me at least! For me the truth was laid bare and from that a saying was born, "the truth is the truth it just wears different clothing"

Now what do I mean by this? What did the light bulb moment actually reveal?

This moment revealed to me the many different levels of truth dependent upon each one's own level of consciousness and where one was at, on their path. How awake or illumined we were, determined the level of "truth" we could possibly conceive, and the language it needed to be communicated in, had to be the language that we spoke at that precise moment in time!!

For me this moment was quite profound and it was a significant stepping stone along my journey to spiritual awakening. I may have not yet found the "magic wand" but had certainly been pointed in the right direction.

A little while after reaching this "light bulb moment" things just started to fall into place so to speak and I was lead through a series of seminars and workshops into some wonderful and life changing friendships. These friendships began or continued the thread of enlightenment that I feel had actually began all those years back when I was growing up on Kangaroo Island.

Through this period in my life I was struggling with financial woes and depression, though my depression was definitely of a high functioning order I was indeed suffering depression (often a resultant side effect of heart attack survival). I was guided to attend a seminar on wealth and the blockages to wealth that may be present in our lives. On this particular seminar I met a beautiful soul by the name of Luci, she was an energetic healer and boy was I in need of some healing! We did a series of healing's where she worked with the energy of Jesus and Mary Magdalen to release blockages within my energy body and she used terms and language that whilst in English, I did not recognise them to be part of any modality I was familiar with. Whilst the healing's certainly helped they were very foreign to me, and I was extremely curious.

After a number of these sessions and much pestering on my behalf, the source, inspiration and training of her modality was revealed to me.

At my therapists Luci's suggestion, I attended a seminar on relationships, hmm ok so what was she trying to tell me? There was nothing wrong with me! It was always their (my ex's) fault not me or mine, I was ok, really! Luci suggested to me that as I had been around energy and energy healing in the past that I would really enjoy the meditations, that I would really feel the energy. Phew, see I knew it wasn't me! So I was just attending to experience meditation? Cool I thought! Luci then mentioned that this was where she had begun her journey as a therapist and that this was where she had learned most of her techniques, and more importantly for my current financial situation, it was being offered by donation. I thought alrighty now we are talking, all the right boxes were being ticked and the ducks were all lined up. I was now intrigued and excited to be attending this seminar called "Empowering Relationships".

Fortunately for me Luci promised me that she would be attending so at least I would know someone, as I had become very insular as a result of my depression.

So along I went, twenty-five people sitting in a lounge room plus two presenters, it was very cozy. Everyone appeared to be quite friendly, warm and welcoming and yes Luci was there! The first day went along very well, I found a comfortable spot to sit after some negotiation, chairs were a prized commodity and I was not a floor dweller! Very soon into the mornings program we did our first meditation and it was as Luci had suggested, I got the energy! Boy did I get the energy! The meditation was a guided meditation and I had done a couple of these in the past, though most of my experience with meditation was of the Buddhist style of mindfulness, of which I was quite proficient. I was able to achieve stillness quite easily and the energy that I experienced that day in the first meditation was some of the most pure and high vibrational energy I had ever felt, it was as I have described to many people since, the "cleanest" energy I had ever experienced.

I was hooked! I hadn't realised it yet, but as I shared this with one of the participants, he quietly explained that the community which was called Shanti Mission, conducted these meditations every week and that he was one of the facilitators, the next meditation was just two days away. Awesome! I obtained the address, just five minutes from my home and as this too was offered by donation, even better!

My other major experience on that weekend was the introduction of a teaching that has become such a profound tool for my understanding of life, the "V diagram". A teaching from Kim Fraser, also known as Sri Shakti Durga, a living Guru based in Australia. This "V diagram" perfectly described to me how everything from my inner knowing and insight into what I considered to be reality, or my perception of reality came to be. All the observations and ideas I had about life and my connection to spirituality and the Divine and how we indeed are all one and connected at some deep cosmic level, all became very clear to me in the instant I saw the teachings.

Wow! Another "light bulb" moment and a significant one at that! For me more proof that "the truth is the truth it just wears different clothing".

During the eighties when I had first begun my exploration into what then was always referred to as the metaphysical, I was introduced to the concept of reincarnation through conversation, reading books around past life regression and being given a copy of a book titled "A Souls Journey" (authored by Peter Richelieu). This book introduced a construct of the evolution of the soul, how our soul has evolved over millennia and what may happen after we pass from this life in human form. So to me the notion of the continuing evolution of the soul through multiple incarnations just made sense, I could not grasp the concept that we only lived just once and that what we did in this life time didn't matter in the greater scheme of things.

The "V diagram " introduced the concept of the multidimensional body or multidimensional existence; that is that we not only exist in the physical body or realm, but that we also exist within an etheric (energetic) body/realm, the astral body/realm, the soul realm and the Divine void.

Now, fortunately I was being exposed to the teachings of Sri Shakti Durga to further expand upon this construct in a way that made complete sense to me. When the student is ready the teacher appears, I was ready!

Also during this seminar, which for me was life changing, I learned about the inner workings of my human existence. I was introduced to the Inner Adult, Parent and Child terms with which I was familiar from previous study in Transactional Analysis and the work of Hal and Vidra Stone into subpersonalities, however this went a little further and with a slightly different bent. We were shown where the Ego fits in this model and its role and the concept that the Inner Parent actually existed as two aspects, that being the Critical Parent (one with which I was quite familiar) and the Nurturing Parent (of which I had nil experience!).

Now the notion of my Ego was familiar to me however as most of us have been taught that "ego is a dirty word", I was surprised to learn from Shakti Durga's teachings that this in fact was not true. Here I learned the role of the ego and its importance in our physical lives in driving the vehicle (so to speak) that is our physical body. I learned that the ego was important in pursuing things that I desired in the physical realm, that it made sure that I presented well and that I looked good and that I was able to compete and be seen. However what I also learned during this time and that I continue to learn to this very day, is that in order to become awakened to my soul's journey and my purpose here on our beautiful mother earth, I had to refine my ego, to befriend it and educate my ego (myself) so that I may move forward upon my journey with humility compassion and forgiveness.

Now this is a process! As the ego identifies itself as being separate; separate from you, separate from nature, separate from the Divine.

How could I possibly achieve this?

Well, it was time for me to take responsibility for myself and my actions and now that I was armed with the understanding of the "V diagram" and how we were all connected as one, a knowing that I had understood from my childhood growing up on the farm on Kangaroo Island, I was ready to embark towards my awakening. This required me to work on the concept taught by Shakti Durga, that is one of the pillars of understanding that the Shanti Mission community aspires to, of one hundred percent personal responsibility!!

Are you for real? Do you mean I cannot blame anyone else for anything that happens to me? Yes correct! Now this concept is huge and requires a lot of work on the ego, the inner child and the inner parent, and is best journeyed with a spiritual mentor and supporting teachings which fortunately I now had. The real key for me to begin this process was an epiphany that I had experienced only a month or so after attending that first seminar with Shanti Mission. It was a massive experience for me. I would like to share this intimate experience with you now.

The Awakening

After my last marriage breakup and the consequent heart attack that ensued, I was very bitter and angry, confused and wallowing in self pity and victim mode. Now I can't do this when practicing one hundred percent personal responsibility. Well I was!

I was sitting alone in my lounge room contemplating life and how sad I felt and I guess I was asking for some form of clarity with what had gone "wrong" thus far, when the blank wall that I was staring became the perfect canvas for my mind to play a movie. In this movie I saw what I perceived at the time to be my former partner and wife and myself in what I knew was the soul realm. We were not in physical form but rather in the form of geometries of light and sound! Here I experienced the contract and agreement that we had made to offer teaching and learning for each other in our next incarnation together. Words really do not adequately allow me the ability to describe what I actually experienced on that night in that moment, other than to say that I understood in an instant why our lives had come together and the deep learning and wisdom teaching that we provided for each other and our children who were also a part of this Divine play.

The enormity of the love that I felt at that moment of illumination was beyond any experience of love that I ever had in my life previously. The scope and depth of feeling truly defies any attempt on my behalf to describe in words. In that instant I felt Divine love, bliss, compassion, humility and an acceptance of and understanding for the purpose, intention and power of forgiveness in my life. Forgiveness of myself and for those who had caused me pain and suffering. I was completely knocked back by what I had experienced. Tears streaming down my face, tears of bliss, comprehension and joy for the Divine and the Divine within me and all beings.

It was profound!

This experience along with more teachings of the tools for self awakening and self love and peace that I learned with Shanti Mission, put me on a path of spiritual practice that has led to my Spiritual Awakening!

Every day for nearly two years during my spiritual practice, I would do forgiveness work. This consisted of chanting and meditation to connect with the divine within me and to open and expand my heart. I was familiar with a process of forgiveness called Ho'oponopono practiced by the Huna culture of Hawaii, brought to prominence to the west by Dr. Hew Len, a psychologist working within the criminal justice system of America. His work is well documented and I had seen a YouTube video of him talking in the past, but did not understand forgiveness as I now understood and felt it, therefore my ego did not allow me to experiment with the practice before. The principal of Ho'oponopono was also taught within Shanti Mission, and I was now at a level of consciousness to begin this practice in earnest.

So every day for nearly two years I practiced forgiveness and chanted in support of this work. The effects of practicing forgiveness within my life, the daily benefits that I am aware of and the observations of my children family and friends as to how much I have changed during this period of time is very humbling. The forgiveness work, whilst I still regularly practice this, led me to greater acceptance of my inner child (my emotions or emotional body) and the desire to learn more about and connect with my inner child.

I had been led, through a dear friend, to the work of Dr John Pollard known as Inner Parenting. Here I began the process of connecting to my inner child through the daily practice of journaling and this has allowed me to become much more attuned to my emotions and my internal guidance and intuition. Learning to become more deeply aware of my emotions, through these and other techniques I have acquired through my journey, has benefited me in many ways, allowing me to operate in my day to day living with harmony, deep peace and balance for the large majority of the time. Mastery of this is a work in progress for now!

In my continued journey and with the awakening of my consciousness and intuition I have come to understand my soul's purpose for this lifetime. Which I believe is firstly to remember who I am as a Divine child of God and to help others attain this same awareness, to awaken to the Divine to be the best that they can be to remember that we are all one, that we journey the same albeit by different paths. My spiritual teacher puts this so eloquently when she describes the spiritual journey we all undertake and the many paths to awakening as "It is all ice-cream, some like vanilla, some chocolate, some cookies and cream, it is all ice-cream, which flavor is yours?"

Finally, it came to me some time ago, perhaps two or three years ago, that for me there appears to be a program that is running in the minds and the subconscious of Humanity. This program is focused around a word that I will describe as a "command word", a word who's meaning energetically is to shape and manipulate the subconscious into a singular outcome. The command word that I describe and refer to here is "FORGET"

Forget is such an insidious and innocuous word whose energy is low vibrational.

- o   Insidious: Adjective; Beguiling but harmful; Intended to entrap.
- o   Innocuous: Adjective; Not causing disapproval.

Notice how many times this is used in our world, in media, in general language, in education especially. How many times do you hear "don't forget to do blah", "Oh before I forget such and such" or "I'll never forget xyz" The command word to use instead in these situations is "REMEMBER"!

Therefore, a more positive response to such situations would be "Remember to do blah", "Oh while I remember such and such" or the big one, "I will always remember xyz". It is my firm belief, though I have not yet completed enough anecdotal research to form a concise opinion, is that indigenous languages around the globe do not have a word or term that actually means forget, for the indigenous cultures around the globe always remember who they are and their connection to the land, Great Spirit and the universe. This has also been a great leap forward in my journey to spiritual awakening, it has played such a significant part in my remembering who I am and why I am here.

I have gained the life benefits that I have from having a spiritual teacher who is a living Guru, coupled with life changing events such as my heart attack, my forgiveness epiphany, meeting and connecting with my Inner Parent, Inner Child, Ego, and Adult aspects of my Self and the significant "light bulb" moment of the "V diagram".

I have lived thus far an exceptional life for which I am unashamedly eternally grateful to all the wonderful people and energies in my life and all the opportunities I have to learn every single day that I take in breath.

This is such a short abbreviated explanation of My Journey to Spiritual Awakening I am honored to share it with you in the hope that it may inspire someone to also seek the truth of who they are and to REMEMBER why they are here.

Namaste

Author Biographies

1. John Spender didn't learn how to read and write at a basic level until he was 10 years old. He has since traveled the world started many business's leading him to create the award winning book series 'A Journey Of Riches', he is an Award Winning International Speaker and Movie Maker. He was an international NLP trainer and has coached thousands of people from various backgrounds through all sorts of challenges. From the borderline homeless to wealthy individuals, John has helped many get in touch with their truths to create a life on their terms.

John's search for answers to living a fulfilling life has take him to working with Native American Indians in the Hills in San Diego, the forests of Madagascar, swimming with humpback whales in Tonga, the Okavango Delta of Botswana and the Great Wall of China. He's travelled from Chile to Slovakia, Hungary to the Solomon Islands, the mountains of Italy and the streets of Mexico. Everywhere his journey has taken him, John has discovered a hunger among people to find a new way to live, together with a yearning for freedom.

He also co-wrote the script for the film 'Adversity and interviewed all the guests.

Website: ajourneyofriches.com

Facebook Page: https://www.facebook.com/AJourneyOfRiches49/

2. Kara is an intuitive healer, Reiki Master and Emotional Well-being coach. She has provided holistic healing to women, men and children in all areas of life, including: addictions, anxiety, depression, parenting, relationships, post-natal care, trauma, self-love and sexual healing.

She also lovingly works as a Doula to support women whilst bringing life into the World. Her gentle, caring and nurturing nature allows others to feel relaxed, loved and safe in her presence. She passionately lives and leads through her strong feminine energy. She creates sisterhood by empowering and connecting women in community to come together and rise in love, celebration and ceremony.

She supports the 'Rise of the Feminine' movement and encourages others to embrace their sacred feminine gifts and to connect to Mother Earth for guidance, wisdom and inner power. She personally enriches others to make conscious choices for a heartfelt, authentic and conscious life.

www.kara-lea.com.au

Connect, Care, Create

3. Scott Cohen is a native of Southern California, married to his wife Merced of 26 years, they've raised two amazing children, Paige and Tanner, who are now in their early twenties. Scott now lives as a leader who is powerful, understanding and vulnerable.

Scott has transformed from intellectualism, to emotional intelligence as a way of being, and heart based decision making. This has served Scott well, plunging into the "gap" actualized his creativity to a whole new level. Now Scott's interactions are heart-to-heart, and Mastery is his way of being.

Scott is a Certified Senior Advisor, Licensed Mortgage and Insurance agent, and has created a National network of service providers, catering to the distribution of one's estate, whether it's a Senior, Baby boomer, Gen X or a Millennial, his Later Life Planning® and Life Planning® systems, create quality of life for your younger years, retirement and beyond, all from abundance.

www.laterlife.us

4. Linda is the founder of BARC, a Practioner of Acupuncture, and a quite a well known artist and song writer/ singer poet.

She has a Diploma of Acupuncture, also post grad diploma in Chinese herbal medicine and a diploma in fine arts, she is the CEO of BARC bali adoption rehabilitation center, in bali.

For twenty years Linda has been picking up making well and adopting pups to good families , BARC rehabilitation center has helped thousands of neglected pups and dogs to new beginnings and hope.

balidogrefuge@gmail.com

or bullergallery@gmail.com

www.barc4balidogs.org.au

5. Michele Cempaka is an internationally renowned Consciousness facilitator, Shaman, Hypnotherapist and author who has been trained to facilitate expansion and deep transformation for others. She utilizes a wide variety of tools to assist her clients with their awakening, healing and profound understanding about themselves and their lives. Michele offers transformational retreats & trainings around the world and in Bali where she lives.

Her extensive experience working abroad gives her work an even greater depth, as she has the ability to facilitate change for people from all walks of life. Michele has lived on Bali since 2002 and integrates the indigenous spiritual qualities within her unique teachings and practice, providing a transformative healing experience for everyone she encounters.

www.spiritweaverjourneys.com

Email: info@spiritweaverjourneys.com

6. After completing art school Julie studied make-up artistry and freelanced in the film and television industry for fifteen years. After the birth of her second son, she formally pursued a career in psychotherapy and completed a master's degree in counselling and applied psychotherapy in 2013. Julie worked clinically for nearly five years in a rehabilitation centre for woman with substance addiction before starting her own psychotherapy/coaching business. She is passionate about and advocates for shifting the stigma associated with sexual, physical and emotional abuse towards women. Julie says she is here to help woman navigate through their trauma and facilitate transformation. She believes women are being called to rise up and re-claim their power and voice as there is no freedom in remaining silent.

To connect with Julie visit: www.consciouscalling.com or email: julie@consciouscalling.com.au

7. Trish Rock | Modern Day Intuitive

Trish is a passionate Speaker & Author, Holistic Counsellor and Psychic with a passion for helping people step into the Light of their own Heart. She transforms lives.

She has a natural ability to intuitively guide her clients to find the best solutions to what may be keeping them from living the life they desire, and deserve.

Connecting to spirit, and with the use of Tarot, Oracle and Numerology as well as using the Chakra Energy System, she is able to find a solution to what is holding people back from living a life of fun, happiness, prosperity and purpose.

Trish is also trained as a Kundalini Reiki Master, Angelic Reiki healer, Holistic Health and WellBeing practitioner, Meditation channel and holds a Post Grad in Mind Body Medicine.

Join Trish Rock's FREE ABUNDANCE CLASS here: http://bit.ly/AbundanceClassroom

Web: www.TrishRock.com

FB: TrishRock7 & TrishRockManifestForLife

Email: trish@trishrock.com

Insta: @trish_rock_7

Twitter: @trishrock7

8. Alexandra's love of people inspires her to support individuals to dream and to move forward from Their CAN'T List to Their CAN List to Success.

As a Result Coach & Mentor with a Holistic approach, her Techniques are unique in assisting individuals achieve their Dreams and Destination.

She's a Speaker, Trainer, Writer, Consultant and Business Owner. In the background, Alexandra also has supported diversity in the industries of human development and Arts in various communities.

www.downundercoaching.com

www.facebook.com/gratitudedreaming

9. Ganga Dev (John Wright), is a qualified Energy Healer, workshop and meditation facilitator, Sacred musician and Kirtan artist and apprentice spiritual teacher. He also holds a Certificate IV in Workplace Training and Assessment, and in his "day job" as a motor vehicle driving instructor is charged with "initiating" Learner drivers into the world by teaching them about 100% responsibility for their actions.

Ganga Dev is passionate about being the best that he can be in his personal and professional life, offering through, experiential workshops, meditation mantra and music a template for embodying the divine into everyday mindfulness and gratitude for life.

He firmly believes that we are here upon this earth to "To awaken and remember who we are through our divinity, and to anchor peace on earth through embodying peace within".

In this compilation book by John Spender "A Journey of Riches" Ganga Dev's chapter "My Journey to Spiritual Awakening" chronicles his personal journey of awakening and remembering his own divinity.

Ganga Dev currently lives in Adelaide, South Australia and can be contacted via Facebook : Ganga Dev or my business page "Ascension Healing & Transformation"

Web www.gangadev.com

Closing words

I hope you enjoyed the collection of heart felt stories, wisdom and vulnerability shared. Story telling is the oldest form of communication and I hope you feel inspired to take a step to living a fulfilling life. Feel free to contact any of the authors in this book or the other books in this series :)

Please help us get the inspiring messages out to people by leaving an honest review on amazon.com and lets have more people living from the mindset that you can truly do anything with this life.

Other books in the series are…

Personal Changes: A Journey Of Riches Book 5

https://www.amazon.com/Personal-Changes-Journey-John-Spender-ebook/dp/B075WCQM4N/

Dealing with Changes in Life: A Journey Of Riches (Self-help guide, Change, Motivational, Inspirational Book 4) https://www.amazon.com/Dealing-Changes-Life-Motivational-Inspirational-ebook/dp/B0716RDKK7/

Making Changes: A Journey Of Riches (Self help guide, Changes, Life changes, Change, Spiritual,

Habits Book 3) https://www.amazon.com/Making-Changes-Journey-changes-Spiritual-ebook/dp/B01MYWNI5A/

The Gift In Challenge: A Journey Of Riches (Self-Help, Anthology Books, Spiritual Solutions, Mindset, Book 2) https://www.amazon.com/Gift-Challenge-Self-Help-Anthology-Spiritual-ebook/dp/B01GBEML4G/

From Darkness into the Light: A Journey Of Riches (Self-Help, Mindset, Motivation, Inspiration, Anthology, Short Stories Book 1) https://www.amazon.com/Darkness-into-Light-Motivation-Inspiration-ebook/dp/B018QMPHJW/

Thank you for all the authors that have shared aspects of their lives in the hope that it will inspire others to live a bigger version of themselves. I heard a great saying from Benjamin J Harvey and that is 'We are only as sick as our secrets' When you share your secrets you just never know who you will inspire and heal in the process.

Also a big shoutout to the editors Ian McAlister, Marina Marsden, Rachel Kupper and Gwendolyn Parker Dodd for making grammatical correctness without losing the voice of the authors.

www.ingramcontent.com/pod-product-compliance
Lightning Source LLC
LaVergne TN
LVHW051827080426
835512LV00018B/2757